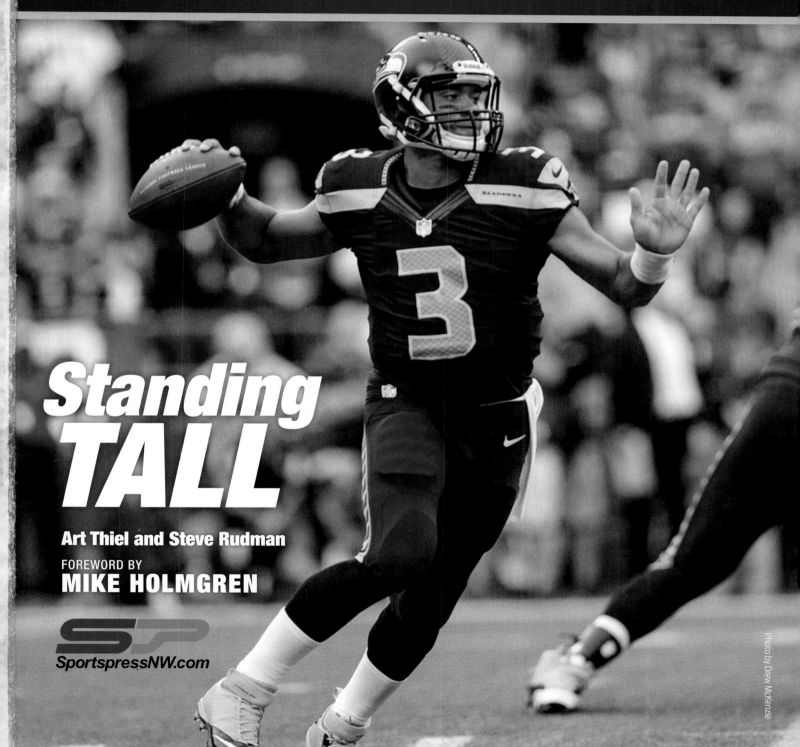

RUSSELL WILSON

Standing **TALL**

Art Thiel and Steve Rudman

FOREWORD BY
MIKE HOLMGREN

SP
SportspressNW.com

Photo by Drew McKenzie

Russell Wilson earned two Pro Bowl berths in his first two seasons with the Seahawks, the first quarterback in franchise history to achieve that feat. (Photo by Drew Sellers)

This book is book is available in quantity at special discounts for your group or organization. For further information, contact:

Triumph Books LLC
814 North Franklin Street
Chicago, Illinois 60610
Phone: (312) 337-0747
www.triumphbooks.com

Printed in U.S.A.
Hardcover ISBN: 978-1-62937-080-4
Paperback ISBN: 978-1-62937-033-0

Sportspressnw.com
Co-Founders: Art Thiel and Steve Rudman
Tim Garrison (technology), Mark Hulak (business), Adam Lewis (reporter)

Content packaged by Mojo Media, Inc.
Joe Funk: Editor
Jason Hinman: Creative Director

Front and back cover photos by Drew McKenzie

Photo by Drew McKenzie

CONTENTS

FOREWORD

By Mike Holmgren

I will admit it: I was one of the skeptics. For years, NFL personnel have used quantitative measures to provide insight into the potential of players, including numbers for height, weight, 40-yard dash time, vertical jump, and bench press, to name a few. Hand-in-hand with these numbers is one of the most prominent NFL truisms: To play in this league, quarterbacks need to be tall.

Historically, successful quarterbacks in the NFL have been tall. Dan Marino is 6'4". John Elway is 6'3". Joe Montana and Brett Favre are 6'2". Boomer Esiason, Jim Kelly, Doug Williams, Troy Aikman, Tom Brady, Donovan McNabb, Ben Roethlisberger—all more than six feet, tall enough to see over their sizable offensive linemen. Only Drew Brees stands out among present and future quarterback greats as falling short of the "necessary" height requirement.

I was at the Cleveland Browns when Russell Wilson entered the 2012 NFL draft, and our scouting department really liked him as a player. He was an all-state quarterback at his high school in Virginia. At the University of Wisconsin, he led his team to a 2012 Big Ten Championship and a Rose Bowl berth. Everyone recognized that he was a really good player. But questions loomed over where he would be taken in the draft.

The problem? He is 5'11".

On draft day, size worked against him. A lot of teams passed on Wilson, until the Seattle Seahawks selected him in the third round. Some news outlets described the Seahawks as "taking a chance" on his ability to play quarterback because of his size.

In return, he beat the odds by leading his team to a Super Bowl victory.

I believe Wilson has become the archetype for why it is necessary to look beyond the statistics to the intangibles that separate the good players from the great players.

Quality of character.

Perseverance to win despite obstacles.

Commitment to studying the opponent.

Heart for the team and the community.

It has been my privilege to get to know Russell during his brief tenure in the NFL. It is clear to me that these are the characteristics that define him, not his size. He displays a remarkable maturity and clarity of purpose.

It is not uncommon to hear stories of him studying film at the facility in the early hours of the morning, only to conclude the day visiting with children at a local hospital or nonprofit organization. He leads his team with his work ethic rather than his words to the press.

At 25, a year removed from his rookie season, he is still learning the game, yet he displays the awareness and understanding of a seasoned veteran. In games when mistakes

can mean the difference between a win and a loss, Wilson doesn't make mistakes.

Fellow skeptics need no more solid evidence than Super Bowl XLVIII, where football fans were treated to storyline after storyline of one of the most prolific NFL quarterbacks of all time: Peyton Manning. The game was supposed to belong to him. Instead the victory went to the upstart, who, with calm efficiency and team play, led Seahawks to victory.

And that is just Wilson the player. It is difficult to believe, but Russell is an even a better person than he is a quarterback. He is really solid. He is exactly the kind of player, as a competitor and a person, a coach wants leading his team.

I have had the privilege of coaching some of the game's great quarterbacks: Joe Montana, Steve Young, Brett Favre, Mark Brunell, Matt Hasselbeck, and others. They led their teams to Super Bowls. They were elected to the Pro Bowl. A few are in the Hall of Fame. I have no doubt that, if he continues on the trajectory of success established in just two seasons, Wilson has a chance to be remembered among the greats. There is no reason to think he won't continue that success.

Russell Wilson has already proved me wrong once. I have learned my lesson. Don't bet against this underdog. ■

During the 2012 season, Russell Wilson had three consecutive games with a passer rating of 125.0 or higher, becoming the first NFL rookie to accomplish that feat. (Photo by Drew McKenzie)

INTRODUCTION

By Art Thiel

Relative to, say, the 13.8 billion-year-old universe, 35 years is not much time. Relative to, say, the Twitterverse, 35 years is equal to 3.386 eternities. Since we in the sports realm are closer to grasping Twitter, it's fair to suggest that the void between major professional sports championships in Seattle was long, dark, and cold.

Which is why Russell Wilson, at 25, deserves a book. He filled the void.

Pro team championships are elusive, especially in Seattle. The 1979 NBA SuperSonics had been the most recent victors—a franchise that no longer exists, at least in the hearts of those in the mossiest corner of the fruited plain. To even get a title chance was rare—the Sonics did again in 1996, when they found in the Finals Michael Jordan and maybe the best team in NBA history, and the 2005 Seahawks, who found the much-beloved Pittsburgh Steelers in Super Bowl XL and official incompetence rarely seen outside North Korea.

That's it. The Mariners? Not so much. They are one of two Major League Baseball teams to have never reached the World Series.

Then on February 2, 2014, at MetLife Stadium in the New Jersey swamplands, the Seahawks, led by Wilson, obliterated the Denver Broncos 43–8. For those witnesses purely interested in dramatic spectacle, the game was a flop. For fans of the Seahawks, it was majestic.

Looming over the depth and breadth of the beat down was an unprecedented experience for Seahawks fans: a favored, well-regarded team throughout the season and playoffs, not only met expectations but it also exceeded them.

Fear of failure is writ large in the Northwest sporting psyche. Always, a trap door awaits. A banana peel sneaks underfoot. The 404 error message appears just before sending.

Not this time. Because the Seahawks were led by a player who always meets and exceeds expectations. So on February 6, 700,000 fans also exceeded expectations by commencing a group hug downtown on a 10-degree day that still elicits grins at the mere mention.

More than any single individual, but not without the help of many, including those known as Twelves, Wilson delivered a title because he did the hardest job well. With singular consistency over two first years in the NFL, Wilson ignored history, skeptics, and large, mean men in opponent jerseys, to concern himself only with the next moment of film study, of practice, of game action. The ability to sustain concentration while chaos erupted around him was an astonishing feat for one so inexperienced.

When the Seahawks visited FedEx Field in suburban Maryland January 6, 2013, the franchise had not won a

playoff game on the road in 29 years. After coming back from down 14–0 to beat Washington 24–14 in front of the largest crowd in Redskins history, fullback Michael Robinson explained his experience in watching Wilson work the game.

"It is a little weird," he said. "To keep his composure in this wild environment, first playoff game for him and all… it's just weird. But Russell Wilson always does it. I've seen veteran, older quarterbacks crumble and crack in the same situation. Not him."

Before and after that surprising game, preposterous feats and outcomes marbled his first two Seahawks seasons in such a compelling fashion that a narrative begged to be assembled in one place. You have it in your hands.

Steve Rudman, cofounder of Sportspress Northwest, and our colleagues Drew Sellers, Drew McKenzie, Adam Lewis, Tim Garrison, and Mark Hulak created the stories and pictures and helped with technology and business. We hope you enjoy.

Russell Wilson will never stand up as high as most in his line of work. Yet he stood out, and on his way to the top, stood conventional pro football wisdom on its head. ◼

Russell Wilson looks on during the Seahawks' October 17, 2013, win over the Arizona Cardinals. With the Seahawks' victory in Super Bowl XLVIII, Wilson became the first quarterback in the Super Bowl era to win 28 games in his first two seasons. (Photo by Drew McKenzie)

CHAPTER 1

BATTLE FOR SEATTLE QB JOB

The Seahawks were highly attracted to Russell Wilson's over-sized hands, a key factor in their decision to select him 75th overall in the 2012 NFL Draft. (Photo by Drew Sellers)

"HE'LL STRUGGLE TO SEE THE (NFL) FIELD IN 3 YEARS."

Skeptics Mock Seahawks' Third Round Draft Pick

Many were mystified when the Seattle Seahawks, selecting in the third round (75th overall) of the 2012 NFL draft, opted for the University of Wisconsin's Russell Wilson. He was a quarterback who, by all reckoning, utterly failed to fit the team's needs. Since the Seahawks had recently guaranteed free agent Matt Flynn $10 million over two years (a $26 million total contract) to become their quarterback of the future, spending a third-round pick on Wilson seemed a curious price to pay for training camp fodder. And that wasn't the real puzzle.

By NFL standards, Wilson was a runt, standing a haircut shy of 5'11"—5'10 5/8", according his measurement at the NFL combine. Why would any NFL team defy widely accepted scouting intelligence and toss away a draft pick on a stumpy quarterback who required elevator shoes and a footstool to converse eye-to-eye with Peyton Manning?

SI.com opined for most when it wrote, "The Seahawks certainly made a questionable decision. Wilson is destined to sit behind newly signed Matt Flynn and will struggle to see the field at any point over the next three years." Most draftniks wouldn't have argued if SI.com had written "three years…if ever."

Pro Football Weekly offered a more generous, although hardly encouraging, analysis, writing, "Wilson might (one day) be sprinkled into a game plan."

Not only did Wilson seem destined to idle behind Flynn, who spent four years backing up Aaron Rodgers in Green Bay, but behind veteran Tarvaris Jackson, Seattle's starting quarterback in 2011. The inevitability of that scenario playing out resonated with all, save the two men who had something to say about it, Wilson and Seattle head coach Pete Carroll.

"People tell me that I'm too short—they've been telling me that my whole life," Wilson said in his first teleconference call with skeptical Seahawks media. "From my perspective, I think the main thing is that I have all the other tools. I have big hands, long arms, and I think the main thing is I have a big heart."

Despite Wilson's exuberance, plus the athletic ability and leadership skills most NFL scouts agreed he possessed, those attributes still seemed insufficient to overcome the sorry history of sub-6-footers in the NFL.

Back to 1952, 36 years before Wilson was born, only two quarterbacks as short, or shorter, produced successful NFL careers as long-term starters: Eddie LeBaron (Washington and Dallas, 1952-63), at 5'7", and Doug Flutie (Chicago, New

Despite his relatively small stature (5'10 5/8"), Russell Wilson attracted the Seahawks' interest in part because of what coach Pete Carroll called "off-the-wall intangibles." (Photo by Drew McKenzie)

England, Buffalo, and San Diego, 1986-2005, as well as nine years in the Canadian Football League) at 5'9³/₄".

In the eight seasons before the Seahawks selected Wilson, 23 quarterbacks were first-round picks, 15 becoming full-time starters. None stood less than six feet all. Over the same span, 82 quarterbacks had been selected in the second round or lower. Only seven had become starters, and all stood more than six feet tall, the group averaging 6'3". But those facts left undaunted Carroll or general manager John Schneider when they watched tape of Wilson's college career.

"Russell has such incredible athleticism and has had historic success," said Carroll, who practically went Gabby Douglas, back-flipping his way through the draft room, after landing Wilson. "He's an extraordinary kid who can handle all the pressure and scrutiny. All he's ever done is be great."

"He's extremely talented and he gains the trust of everyone around him," added Schneider. "He can tilt a room."

But could Wilson tilt a playing field?

A native of Richmond, Virginia, Wilson graduated in three years from North Carolina State, where he became the first freshman named All-ACC first-team quarterback. He played baseball well enough that two major league teams, the Baltimore Orioles (41ˢᵗ round, 2007) and Colorado Rockies (fourth round, 2010), drafted him. Wilson played second base in Colorado's minor league system in 2011-12, but not long after his father died, he decided to play football again, transferring to Wisconsin for his final year of college eligibility.

Schneider and Carroll saw that Wilson was voted team captain by his new Badgers teammates. It took him three weeks to master Wisconsin's playbook. Six months after arriving in Madison, Wilson had the Badgers in the Rose Bowl opposite Oregon after leading an offense that averaged 44.6 points.

Wilson participated in his first Seahawks mini-camp in May 2012. It took Carroll three days to make the ground shift at the Virginia Mason Athletic Center, the suburban Renton facility where the Seahawks trained and once the site of a coal tar refinery. Asked at the end of camp where Wilson fit into Seattle's quarterback picture, Carroll surprised by declaring an "open competition" for the job.

"Here's what I'm going to say about it," Carroll told reporters. "Wilson's going to be in the competition. He showed us enough. This is going to tax us. It was already going to be taxing with two quarterbacks (Flynn and incumbent Jackson). But we already know he can throw. He's got a great arm. He did an excellent job of demonstrating that he's prepared for this."

The question was whether Carroll was guilty of another burst of over-the-top enthusiasm while overlooking Wilson's obvious shortcoming—Carroll had, after all, once waxed eloquent over nondescript Charlie Whitehurst—or whether Carroll and the Seahawks were really on to something. Smooth and articulate, Wilson used a post-minicamp interview to beat back doubters.

"I played in two great, great conferences in the ACC and the Big 10," Wilson said. "I've shown that I can play at a very high level and be very productive with the football. I think the main thing is just being efficient, being a facilitator of the football and getting there to work every single day and compete."

Nice words. But the Seahawks had not agreed to pay Flynn, who once threw for 480 yards and six touchdowns against Detroit while subbing for Aaron Rodgers, to watch from the sidelines. So it was Flynn's job to lose more than Wilson's to win. And if Flynn had lost, Jackson had won 17 of 34 NFL starts on mostly mediocre teams. Could a sub-six-foot rookie really compete with that? ■

When the Seahawks selected Russell Wilson 75ᵗʰ overall in the 2012 NFL draft, he became the highest quarterback taken by the club since Brock Huard went 77ᵗʰ overall in 1999. (Photo by Drew McKenzie)

EXHIBITION GAMES DON'T COUNT, EXCEPT...

Wilson Quick to Seize Preseason Chance

Russell Wilson slammed shut Pete Carroll's "open competition" in the span of two halves and one preseason start. He turned the luckless Matt Flynn, waiting five years for a starting opportunity, into one of the most expensive backups (guaranteed $10 million) in the league. He turned incumbent Tarvaris Jackson into a QB looking for a new team.

For Seattle's first preseason game August 11 against the Tennessee Titans at CenturyLink Field, Carroll named Flynn the starter, Wilson the backup, and Jackson a spectator. Despite Carroll's supportive remark, "We know what T-Jack can do," that also meant he knew what T-Jack couldn't do and wanted an upgrade. The three-way competition had been reduced to Flynn vs. Wilson—unless both flopped.

"I want good information on these two so I can make a clear-cut choice," Carroll said. "Matt has done a fantastic job. He's learned the system, he reads defenses, he moves well. Now I need to see him in a situation where he takes over."

Flynn looked sharp on his first series, going 6-for-6 for 27 yards, and finished 11-for-13 for 71. But he sabotaged a red-zone scoring opportunity with an interception Titans linebacker Colin McCarthy returned into Seattle territory.

Wilson wasted little time topping Flynn. The rookie nimbly scrambled out of the pocket on his first third-and-long and found Charly Martin for a 14-yard completion and a first down. Two plays later, he launched a deep ball down the left sideline intended for Braylon Edwards. The wide receiver leaped over Tennessee's cornerback to haul in a 39-yard touchdown. Wilson finished his first drive 3-for-3 with 59 yards and his first NFL touchdown pass.

Wilson orchestrated two more scoring drives, one ending in a 40-yard Steven Hauschka field goal, the other capped by Wilson with a 32-yard touchdown scramble on a reverse bootleg. Wilson finished his first pro game 12-for-16 for 124 yards, his only mistake a poorly thrown, end-zone interception.

The consensus: Flynn displayed more polish—nothing surprising there—but Wilson seemed to have a more intriguing upside.

Exhibition results are often inconclusive, but after two fake affairs Carroll found himself on the edge of a quarterback controversy. In the second preseason game against Peyton Manning and the Denver Broncos, Flynn, the presumed starter, directed three field goal drives in the first half but had yet to be involved in a preseason touchdown. The

Russell Wilson was considered an afterthought when the Seahawks selected him in the third round of the 2012 NFL Draft, but he quickly won an "open competition" with Matt Flynn and Tarvaris Jackson to become Seattle's starting quarterback. (Photo by Drew McKenzie)

year before, red zone problems had been Jackson's undoing.

Three of Wilson's second-half drives against Denver resulted in touchdowns. But it was the way those touchdowns came about that generated buzz. His ability to turn potentially negative plays into positives bordered on the uncanny. Most notable: A third-down play in the third quarter with the Seahawks up 16-10 en route to a 30-10 victory.

Wilson found himself in the clutches of a Broncos pass rusher and falling down, yet managed to loft an eight-yard pass to the sideline that was caught by Lavasier Tuinei for a first down at the Denver 34. Two plays later, Wilson flipped a quick screen to Tyrell Sutton who, despite an absence of blockers, weaved through the Broncos' defense for a touchdown and a 23–10 lead.

Wilson completed 10 passes in 17 attempts for 155 yards and two touchdowns, while adding 37 rushing yards, all on plays in which he was flushed from the pocket. Carroll couldn't help but notice that all five TDs in the Seahawks' 2–0 preseason start were under the direction of Wilson, who acted in his first two games as if he owned the joint, knowing when and where to run, unloading the ball out of bounds when needed, and showing the stones to match his accuracy in tight windows downfield.

Carroll wasn't quite ready to declare the "open competition" over, acutely aware that making the leap to a rookie QB starter was way out there on the NFL frontier. In the decade before the Seahawks drafted Wilson in the third round, 34 quarterbacks were taken in the first round; only three were named to start as early as August.

So when Carroll named Wilson to start Seattle's third preseason game against Kansas City, he made sure to emphasize the elevation wasn't permanent.

"We are going to give Russell a chance to start," Carroll said. "Matt has done very well and (we're) very pleased, but there's a difference playing with the ones and the twos, really, from the pressure that's generated. But I don't think we will see anything different than what we have been seeing."

Without issuing negatives against Flynn, Wilson's teammates embraced his ascension to No. 1, even if the move proved temporary.

"He's playing at a level you don't expect a rookie to be at right now," said center Max Unger. "There are expectations for a guy you take higher in the draft—not saying third isn't high—but you just don't expect a guy taken in the third round to be in the running for the starting spot right away. To be in the competition this late says what he's done in camp."

"Russell wants to be the best," added Seahawks wide receiver Golden Tate. "From the day I met him, he's been the first one in and the last one out. In meetings, he asks very good questions. Watching the game, you can see the kid is good, but he has worked so hard to get there. He's so driven to be the guy for us."

Starting Wilson against the Chiefs was Carroll's only way to find out the limits of the young quarterback's precociousness—even if a favorable result would complicate his life, and Flynn's. ■

Matt Flynn came to the Seahawks with the expectation that he would become Seattle's starting quarterback. But he lost the job to Russell Wilson during the team's 2012 training camp. (Photo by Drew McKenzie)

ROOKIE VAULTS VETS

Carroll Defies Conventional NFL Wisdom with Wilson

As significant Northwest debuts go, Seahawks rookie quarterback Russell Wilson fell about a dinghy short of Capt. George Vancouver. As for Matt Flynn…he seemed like the guy who came to town the day after the circus left.

Given permission to run with the ones, Wilson acted 33 instead of 23. Against a good Kansas City defense in the hostile road house of Arrowhead Stadium, Wilson made Pete Carroll, the guy out there on the high wire, look like Karl Wallenda.

One half doesn't make a career…does it?

After recording scores on six of the eight possessions he directed in the first two preseason games, Wilson took the first unit to scores on its first six possessions—three field goals, three touchdowns—and defense and special teams added a touchdown each to crush the Chiefs, 44–14.

In a word, it was astonishing. Preseason, yes. But Wilson even made doddering wide receiver Terrell Owens look good (two catches).

"I'm just excited to watch him play," Carroll told reporters. "He continues to show poise and composure well beyond three games. Honestly, this is what we had hoped to see. We saw what he did the first two games, and wanted to see if he could do it again. He was very comfortable for the most part, took off (running) when he needed to. We also wanted to see what happened if he hung in the pocket."

It was almost all good. Wilson completed 13-of-19 passes for 185 yards and two touchdowns for a QB rating of 134.8, plus two scrambles that picked up 59 yards. And no turnovers. Wilson wasn't perfect, but he was beyond good for a rookie—and a third-rounder at that—in his first start. In the absence of Flynn, Tarvaris Jackson saw his first action of the preseason in the second half, completing three of five passes for a single yard.

After an off-season of public debate and controversy about the quarterback spot, Wilson made it easy for Carroll to determine his regular-season starter, even though he said nothing about it after his team ran amok over the Chiefs, the rout aided by touchdowns from safety Earl Thomas on a 75-yard interception return and Golden Tate's 92-yard punt return.

Flynn, the presumptive starter after he signed a three-year, $26 million free agent deal to leave Green Bay in the off-season, was held out of the game because of a sore elbow. But after Wilson sucked up all the lights on Broadway, even good health wouldn't have helped Flynn.

Despite his injury, Flynn looked solid in the preseason. But few other than Carroll and general manager John Schneider, who sold Carroll on Wilson after watching the young quarterback at Wisconsin, figured on Wilson's transcendence. Beyond his passing accuracy, Wilson's ability to turn failing plays into positive ones continued to distinguish him.

Through the 3–0 preseason start, Wilson completed 35-of-52 passes for 464 tards, five touchdowns, one interception, and 150 yards rushing. At 5'11", Wilson was

"He expects to be good. He expects to make plays. That's just the way he is and thinks. Nothing else ever enters his mind. He came to win this job." — Seattle head coach Pete Carroll after naming Russell Wilson his starting quarterback. (Photo by Drew Sellers)

supposed to be too short, but Carroll saw what he'd needed to see. Four days after his performance against the Chiefs, he named Wilson his starting quarterback for the regular-season opener at Arizona.

"It's been a very exciting competition and Russell has taken full advantage of his opportunities and done everything we could ask for on the field," said Carroll. "What he's done off the field, in meeting rooms and how he's represented himself, he's earned this job. When I told him, he was absolutely in stride. I don't think it's going to bother him a bit. He expects to be good. He expects to be successful. He expects to make plays. That's just the way he is and thinks. Nothing else even enters his mind. He came to win this job."

"I don't surprise myself, I think, because I prepare in

the right way," Wilson said after his ascension to No. 1. "I try to visualize myself being very, very successful, and just positive self-talk, I guess."

Carroll's choice of Wilson capped a stunning rise for a quarterback who lasted until the third round in the April draft, the fifth quarterback taken. He seemed destined to be Seattle's third quarterback and a spectator observing the battle between incumbent Jackson and veteran newcomer Flynn.

Instead, Carroll's "open competition" ended with the upstart at No. 1, Flynn at No. 2 and Jackson sent to Buffalo for an undisclosed draft choice. Carroll offered one prescient footnote.

"In time, as you watch him more, you'll come to appreciate the uniqueness of Russell Wilson and his approach." ■

Above: Since the Seahawks ran their offense primarily through running back Marshawn Lynch, the Seahawks did not ask Russell Wilson to do too much as he transitioned from college into the National Football League. Opposite: "I don't surprise myself, I think, because I prepare in the right way. I try to visualize myself being very, very successful, and just positive self-talk, I guess" – Russell Wilson, after he won the Seahawks' starting quarterback job. (Photos by Drew Sellers)

CHAPTER 2

AIMING FOR THE TOP

Russell Wilson speaks with reporters during North Carolina State's media day before the 2010 season. The quarterback played three seasons for the Wolfpack before transferring to Wisconsin in 2011. (AP Images)

IT'S NOT HEIGHT, IT'S HANDS

What the Seahawks Saw Beyond Height

There were other sports stories in the headlines in Seattle during 2012, but Russell Wilson quickly became the biggest one.

On August 15, 2012, Felix Hernandez orchestrated one of the great athletic spectacles in Seattle's 45-year association with professional sports, pitching a perfect game for the Mariners under sunny skies at Safeco Field. King Felix fanned 12 flailing Tampa Bay Rays in his 1–0 perfecto, the 23rd in baseball history and—astonishingly—the third no-hitter at Safeco that summer.

On April 21, Philip Humber, a White Sox journeyman best known as one of four prospects that the Mets traded to Minnesota for Johan Santana in 2008, befuddled the Mariners with a 4–0 perfect game. The Mariners responded June 8 when a journeyman of their own, Kevin Millwood, and five relievers unconventionally collaborated on a no-hitter against the Los Angeles Dodgers.

Before, during, and for several days after King Felix made baseball history, his ongoing saga ranked No. 1 on Seattle's summer must-read list. But after rookie Russell Wilson won the job as the Seahawks' starting quarterback in an open competition with presumed No. 1 Matt Flynn and incumbent Tarvaris Jackson, Wilson quickly eclipsed King Felix as the No. 1 sports story in town. Nothing energizes Seattle sports, not even a perfect game, as much as the prospect of a new quarterback.

Wilson came on with such a blur, through mini-camp, organized team activities, and three preseason games, that he morphed into a region-wide celebrity before anyone knew much about him. Didn't matter.

Radio talk shows buzzed with excitement—and debate. Wilson, some argued, was the most exciting player the Seahawks had signed in years. No, others retorted, once defenses game-planned against him, he wouldn't get away with what he did in preseason. True, he might have a high quarterback aptitude, but making him a starter and exposing him to the large, skilled, mean men of NFL defenses so soon was folly.

Plus, did you hear he was short?

Wilson would become the first rookie quarterback to open a season for the Seahawks since Rick Mirer in 1993. After a passable first year in which the Seahawks asked virtually nothing of Mirer involving the playbook, the Notre Dame grad soon faded into a semi-bust.

Playing for a team in which defense came first, a running game led by Marshawn Lynch came second, and the passing game tied for third with special teams, the Seahawks wouldn't ask much of Wilson early. Having wisely idiot-proofed themselves at the game's key position, they could afford the luxury.

What coach Pete Carroll and general manager John Schneider knew, what they were supremely confident

Russell Wilson was drafted by the Colorado Rockies in the fourth round of the 2010 draft and played minor league baseball in the Rockies' organization for two seasons. In 2011, the second baseman batted .228 in 61 games with the Asheville Tourists. (AP Images)

about, as Carroll's frequent press statements emphasized, was Wilson's ability to negotiate the learning curve faster than most rookies. Being quick on the uptake had always been a Wilson asset.

Born in Cincinnati on November 29, 1988, when Boomer Esiason and Ickey Woods were leading the Bengals to Super Bowl XXIII, Russell Carrington Wilson grew up in Richmond, Virginia, son of Harrison Benjamin Wilson III, a lawyer, and Tammy T. Wilson, a legal nurse consultant.

Wilson's father played football and baseball for Dartmouth in the 1970s. His grandfather, Harrison B. Wilson Jr., played football and basketball at Kentucky State in the 1950s. His great-great grandfather labored for the Confederacy as a slave until freed after the Civil War.

Wilson, who first picked up football at age four, attended Collegiate School, a prep academy in Richmond, first making All-State as a sophomore in 2004. As a junior in 2005, with the Seahawks en route to their first Super Bowl, Wilson threw for 3,287 yards and 40 touchdowns and ran for 634 yards and 15 touchdowns, earning *The Richmond Times-Dispatch's* accolade as state Player of the Year.

He won the award again as a senior in 2006, when he threw 34 touchdowns and ran for 1,132 yards and 18 touchdowns.

Wilson was also elected senior class president, the combination of his athletics and academics earning him a scholarship to Duke. Eschewing that stretch of Tobacco Road, Wilson hoped to attend the University of Virginia. But his height, or lack thereof, scared off recruiters. So he committed to North Carolina State, where he took his redshirt year in 2007, but played the infield for the Wolfpack baseball team.

A year later, Wilson threw for 1,955 yards and 17 touchdowns—with just one interception—and led the Wolfpack to the PapaJohns.com Bowl against Rutgers. The Atlantic Coast Conference named him its first-team All-ACC quarterback, the first time in the conference's history that a freshman was selected first team.

In 2009, Wilson set an NCAA record by completing 379 consecutive passes without an interception. A year later, Wilson led the ACC in passing yards per game (274.1) and total offense (297.5). He also earned a communications

degree in just three years and took graduate-level business courses during the fall semester of the 2010 football season.

Wilson played football, basketball, and baseball at Collegiate School, but dropped basketball when he entered North Carolina State. He showed enough as a high school second baseman that the Baltimore Orioles selected him in the 2007 June draft (41st round). Wilson didn't sign, preferring to pursue a college education, but three years later agreed to a $200,000 contract with the Colorado Rockies when they selected him in the fourth round of the June draft.

By 2010, after Wilson completed enough credits to graduate, he reported to spring training with the Rockies and played 32 games for the Short A Tri-City Dust Devils, a Northwest League entry based in Pasco, Washington. Wilson's football coach, Tom O'Brien, was uncomfortable with Wilson's decision because he missed spring football. After Wilson opted for a second year of minor league baseball, with the Class A Asheville Tourists of the South Atlantic League, instead of spring football, O'Brien began developing other quarterbacks for the 2011 season.

Wilson's commitment to baseball led to an uncomfortable split with North Carolina State's football program. Although Wilson had one year of college eligibility remaining, O'Brien released him from his football scholarship. At about the same time, O'Brien reached out to his NFL contacts to gauge their interest in Wilson, also eligible for the NFL draft.

The 5'11" quarterback/second baseman failed to receive an invitation to the 2011 scouting combine in Indianapolis.

Not much of a hitter (.229 batting average in 93 games), Wilson decided his future was in football. He considered using his final year of eligibility at Auburn, which he visited, but instead committed to Wisconsin on June 27, 2011. In an ESPN interview, Wilson cited Wisconsin's "coaching staff, the program's tradition, and enthusiasm of fans" as reasons for his decision. Almost as soon as he donned a Badgers uniform, Wilson started racking up votes as the greatest one-year wonder in Wisconsin football history.

In the season opener against UNLV, Wilson dropped 51 points on the Rebels, throwing for 255 yards and two touchdowns. He also rushed for 62, including a 46-yard

Russell Wilson did a little bit of everything during his one season at Wisconsin, including catching a 32-yard pass from Montee Ball during the 2011 Big Ten championship game. (AP Images)

touchdown. Wisconsin started the year 6–0 as the Badgers outscored opponents 301–58. At the end of the regular season, 33 touchdown passes later, Wilson was named first-team All-Big Ten, won the Griese-Brees Big Ten Quarterback of the Year award, was selected third-team All-America by Yahoo Sports and finished ninth in Heisman Trophy voting.

In the inaugural Big Ten Championship game December 3, Wilson fired three touchdown passes in a 42–39 win over Michigan State and was named the game's (Red) Grange-(Archie) Griffin MVP. Although Wisconsin lost 45–38 to Oregon in the Rose Bowl, Wilson accounted for 314 yards and three touchdowns (two passing, one running).

By the time he used up his eligibility, Wilson started 50 consecutive games to become the fifth quarterback in college history to pass for more than 5,000 yards (11,720) and rush for more than 1,000 (1,427). In his one year at Wisconsin, he completed 72.8 percent of his passes and set the single-season FBS record for passing efficiency at 191.8, becoming a finalist for several national trophies, including the Manning, Maxwell, Davey O'Brien, and Johnny Unitas Golden Arm awards.

Nearly every 2012 draft evaluator slotted Wilson as a mid-round pick, including ESPN Monday Night Football analyst Jon Gruden, who said, echoing widespread sentiment, "The only issue with Russell Wilson is his height. That might be the reason he's not picked in the first couple of rounds."

"If he was 6'5", he'd probably be the No. 1 overall pick in the draft," added Chris Weinke, director of the IMG Madden Football Academy and the 2000 Heisman Trophy winner.

During the combine in Indianapolis, under the headline "Day 3 Risers and Fallers," *The New York Times* posted a blog that said, "Wilson is a superb athlete, but he is very inconsistent as a passer. He is shorter than Kellen Moore, and several of his passes tend to sail high. Those passes will turn into interceptions at the next level. When he's rolling out, his accuracy also leaves a lot to be desired."

Pro Football Weekly, a chronicler of the sport for decades, summarized Wilson:

"An instinctive, multi-sport athlete with a terrific work ethic and likable personality, Wilson has nearly everything you desire intangibly, including toughness, competitiveness and leadership…Never will be a prototypical dropback, pocket passer, as his height always will be a limiting factor, but he has the arm, legs and smarts to grow into an effective backup…"

Stanford's 6'3" Andrew Luck and Baylor's 6'2" Robert Griffin III went No. 1 and No. 2 in the 2012 draft. But Wilson had one measurable, not lost on the Seahawks, that topped both—his hand span. Wilson's measured 10¼ inches to Luck's 10 inches and Griffin's 9½.

Among the first to notice Wilson's massive paws: Jim Zorn, a long-time NFL coach and the first rookie (1976) quarterback to start an opening game for the Seahawks.

"Russell Wilson's hands are a God-given thing—something you couldn't even design," said Zorn. "If it gets wet and slimy, the grip won't be an issue."

Wilson's hand span was not only larger than Luck's and Griffin's, it was larger than 6'6" Cam Newton's 9 $^{7}/_{8}$ and 6'4" Colin Kaepernick's 9 $^{1}/_{8}$. In fact, it was also larger, by an eighth of an inch, than Robert Quinn's 10 $^{1}/_{8}$. The 6'4", 270-pound defensive end for the St. Louis Rams was selected 14th overall in the 2011 draft.

So while Wilson may have lacked stature, his oversized hands trumped that negative, one of the determining factors in Carroll and Schneider selecting him in the third round.

Schneider admitted as much after the draft, explaining he first noticed Wilson's grip during Wilson's senior year at Wisconsin. Schneider trekked to a Badgers game against Penn State.

"A really nasty, cold, rainy day, and he lit it up," said Schneider. "It wasn't close."

Schneider returned to Seattle and sold Carroll on the merits of selecting Wilson in the third round. Although height-challenged, Wilson possessed every other quality a team would seek: leadership (class president, multiple times a team captain), intelligence (fast-tracked his degree from N.C. State), work habits (first one in, last one out) decision-making skills (few interceptions)—and those massive mitts.

Even so, would it translate on Sundays? ■

Russell Wilson celebrates after Wisconsin defeated Michigan State in the 2011 Big Ten championship game to earn a berth in the Rose Bowl. Wilson led the Badgers to 11 wins during his only season in Madison. (AP Images)

THE FASTEST ROUTE TO THE TOP

Baseball or Football? Wilson Makes a Tough Choice

After Russell Wilson left behind professional baseball to continue his college football career, he wrote a letter to Wisconsin head coach Bret Bielema, explaining he wanted to spend his final year of eligibility playing for the Badgers. Wilson informed Bielema he intended win a Big Ten title, become the conference quarterback of the year, and take Wisconsin to the Rose Bowl. Wilson faxed the letter to Bielema and within six months checked off every item on his list.

Wilson never shared, publicly at least, how he planned to become the Seahawks' starting quarterback, or if he had put himself on a timetable. But when it happened after his preseason performance against Kansas City, the least surprised person in the sports world was Wilson. His coach, Pete Carroll, confirmed that multiple times, in a myriad of ways.

Perhaps no one else thought so, but Wilson harbored such a belief in his unrelenting work habits that he convinced himself he was headed for big things fast. That weighed heavily on the decision to abandon baseball after he was taken in the fourth round, 140th overall, in the 2010 draft by the Colorado Rockies.

Baseball, he recognized, would take him longer to get where he felt he belonged—the top.

"It was one of those things where I had an unbelievable opportunity, but I also had to take an unbelievable risk," Wilson said of giving up pro baseball to return for a final year of college football. "It was extremely tough. I was competing with myself, trying to figure out what was best for my life and what I needed to do. I was just very relaxed and I prayed about it and trusted in the Lord that he would guide me in the right direction. I knew I was going to end up being successful just because of the hard work that I put into it.

"I still had a long way to go (in professional baseball). You have to go through the minor league levels. At the same time, I knew I had this other thing waiting for me in football. If I didn't do that, I knew I would have regretted it for the rest of my life just because I would never have known what I could have done in the NFL.

"I definitely had starting as a goal," Wilson said after his elevation. "I have high expectations of myself. I always have, always will. That will never waver. I always believe in my talent, always have."

Imbued with the confidence that comes from talent, and never afraid to excel, Wilson made it a goal to be great every time he stepped onto a football field. It had nothing to do with swagger, but simply believing in and making use of his tools.

Besides his strong Christian beliefs, Wilson used his smaller stature as a motivational tool. He looked at impediments and saw opportunities.

"Me being a shorter quarterback, I believe I'm playing for a lot of other kids in the future, to be honest with you. That's part of my motivation."

Despite his short stature—5'10 $^5/_8$"—and third-round draft status, Russell Wilson never had any doubt that he would start— and star—in the National Football League. (Photo by Drew McKenzie)

Short-guy syndrome? No. Third-round syndrome? No.

"Not at all. I don't play for other people or anything like that. I play for an audience of one. My viewpoint on (the nay-sayers) is people are going to have their opinions. That's part of the game. They get paid to do that.

"Part of my thing is to do what I can control. Put the best foot forward I can, and just play to the highest level I can possibly play."

Wilson was not any more surprised that he won an open competition to become the Seahawks starting quarterback than he was when everything he set out to do in his year at Wisconsin came true.

"I truly believe in positive synergy, that your positive mindset gives you a more hopeful outlook. A belief that you can do something great means you will do something great," said Wilson, whose first order of business in Seattle was to become the starting quarterback.

"Was I surprised? I was more…so excited about the

opportunity. I felt like I put a lot of hard work in. Matt (Flynn) is a great player too and…just to have the opportunity to help lead this football team is huge. Even though I'm a rookie, I believe in the fact that I can help this team win and do a lot of great things.

"My thing is—and I've always been this way—to get to know as many people as I possibly can on a personal level. That way, when you get on the football field, you've got your buddy right beside you and you're ready to go.

"I don't try to win people over or anything like that. I just try to be myself. Get here early, leave late. The biggest thing is staying a little bit extra, staying a little bit later at night…Mentally, just making sure I go through my checklist and everything I go through every week—the third downs, the pressure looks and the first- and second-down stuff, red zone, two-minute situations. That's what I want to do, that's what I desire to do. I desire to be great." ■

Above: With the Seahawks' offense running through Marshawn Lynch (taking handoff), the Seahawks were afforded the luxury of not throwing too much too soon at Russell Wilson. Opposite: After his nearly flawless play through Seattle's first three 2012 preseason games, Russell Wilson took over as the Seahawks' starting quarterback, becoming the first rookie to win the job since Rick Mirer in 1993. (Photos by Drew McKenzie)

CHAPTER 3

CAUTIOUS START, FLASHY FINISH

Russell Wilson races past a blur of Green Bay Packers during Seattle's 14–12 victory September 24, 2012. Wilson carried three times for 18 yards. (Photo by Drew McKenzie)

CLIMBING THE LEARNING CURVE

Slow Start Transforms Into Big Production

Although excited about Russell Wilson's potential, Pete Carroll did not want to throw too much too soon at his 23-year-old quarterback. The Seahawks had an exceptional runner in Marshawn Lynch and a potentially superb defensive unit, so Carroll did not ask Wilson to do much more than manage games and try to minimize mistakes. Carroll's approach more or less went according to plan.

In Week 1 at Arizona, Wilson almost produced a Hollywood ending, but struggled in the red zone. Three times the Seahawks began drives inside the Cardinals 35-yard line and three times came away with field goals. In the final drive, with Seattle trailing 20–16, Wilson completed 7-of-9 passes before the first of two Arizona pass interference penalties gave the Seahawks a first down at the Arizona 13 with 52 seconds left.

But the shortened field took a toll on Wilson's inexperience. His final five passes, all into the end zone and targeted at four receivers, fell incomplete. Wilson shouldered the blame.

"I have to go through my reads quicker, that's the main thing," said Wilson, who finished 18-for-34 for 153 yards, a touchdown, and a pick. "In the red zone, the windows are a lot shorter and I have to be smarter."

Mostly, Wilson just had to learn. In his first few weeks in the league, there were lots of ups and downs.

Wilson produced his first 100.0-plus passer rating (112.7) in the Week 2 27–7 win over the Dallas Cowboys at Century-Link Field when he had a nearly perfect game from Carroll's perspective: 15 completions in 20 attempts for 151 yards and no turnovers, including a 22-yard touchdown to Anthony McCoy that completed a 90-yard drive in eight plays.

"The quarterback," said Carroll, his usual bundle of enthusiasm, "played really smart and didn't give up the ball. All of those things are emblematic of what we're shooting for."

Wilson delivered his first two-touchdown game (no interceptions) in a Week 3, Monday Night game against Green Bay at the Clink. The game quickly became one of the most memorable of the NFL regular season because it ended on Wilson's 24-yard Hail Mary pass—or "Fail Mary," as it became known nationally—to Golden Tate as the clock expired, giving Seattle a hugely controversial 14–12 win.

Although the result was wildly disputed—many insisted the call was an interception by Packers safety M.D. Jennings instead of a touchdown—and led to the NFL settling a labor dispute that ended the use of replacement referees who made the call, Wilson had two major takeaways from the game: The first fourth-quarter comeback win of his NFL career and the first victory over a Super Bowl-winning quarterback, Aaron Rodgers (Wilson had a 99.3 passer rating to Rodgers' 81.5).

A week later in St. Louis, however, the wheels came off. Wilson threw three interceptions without a touchdown, compiling a dismal 45.8 passer rating, in a 19–13

Russell Wilson (center), a third-round draft choice out of the University of Wisconsin, made the first start of his NFL career September 9, 2012, at Arizona in University of Phoenix Stadium. (Photo by Drew McKenzie)

loss in the Edward Jones Dome.

"I still think he's improving and getting more comfortable," Carroll said after the Rams beat the Seahawks for just the second time in 15 games. "We'll see what it all means. I don't know yet."

The Seahawks went 4–4 in Wilson's first eight games, in which he threw 10 touchdown passes and eight interceptions, including two at Carolina in Week 5. In back-to-back games, Wilson had five picks vs. one touchdown, plunging the Seahawks to a No. 29 league ranking in total offense.

Question: When a team is ranked 29th in offense, when is there not a quarterback controversy? Answer: When the team has a second quarterback over which to have a controversy. According to Carroll, the Seahawks didn't. Matt Flynn was sort-of not available with a vaguely injured elbow.

As Carroll explained, Wilson's interceptions were more on others than him. Although Wilson needed to find

his checkdown receivers faster and make better decisions about when to run, those issues were compounded by protection failures as well as the absence of game-changing plays from receivers, making a hash of the Seattle offense.

Wilson gave perhaps the most telling glimpse into what was to come in Seattle's 16–12 escape from Carolina in a homecoming of sorts. Wilson played three seasons at nearby North Carolina State.

After throwing an ill-advised pass that Captain Munnerlyn returned 33 yards for a Panthers touchdown, Wilson, on a third-and-8 from the Carolina 13 with 35 seconds left in the third quarter, responded by rocketing a pass to Tate for a touchdown for what proved to be the winning points.

It marked just Seattle's fourth TD of the season in 14 trips to the red zone. Wilson, who entered the game with a 45.5 rating on third down, never threw a better NFL pass. That was about to change. ■

Above: Russell Wilson threw a pair of touchdown passes in leading the Seahawks to a 14–12 victory over the Green Bay Packers at CenturyLink Field on September 24, 2012. Opposite: Taking the handoff from Russell Wilson, Marshawn Lynch ran for 118 yards and a touchdown at St. Louis on September 30, 2012, but the Seahawks suffered a 19–13 loss to the Rams. (Photos by Drew McKenzie)

THE TURN BEGINS

Wilson Out-Does Brady as Seahawks Stun Patriots

Not often in the NFL does the No. 1-ranked offensive team bump helmets with the No. 1 defensive team. It hadn't happened in Week 6 or later since December 9, 2007, when the New England Patriots, the best offensive team, defeated the Pittsburgh Steelers. Not even close—New England rolled, 34–13.

On October 14, 2012, New England arrived at CenturyLink Field, again the NFL's No. 1 offense, averaging 33 points, to face a Seahawks defense ceding a league-low 10.8. While the Patriots defense ranked 24th, it didn't figure to have much difficulty shutting down a Seahawks offense that ranked 25th (31st in passing). Without one-man rampage Marshawn Lynch, Seattle wouldn't have had any offense at all.

But in one of the most dramatic regular-season home games in Seahawks history, little Russell Wilson, looking more like big Tom Brady, fired two touchdown passes in the game's final seven minutes to overcome a 23–10 deficit and produce a dumbfounding 24–23 triumph that defied all sorts of NFL gravity.

This time, no asterisks had to be applied because of replacement refs, responsible for a bad call in the Green Bay game on Golden Tate's "Fail Mary" touchdown. This time, no one questioned the Seahawks' ability, integrity, or fortune. The only external factor was booster rockets applied by 68,137 adherents who stood in the rain, screaming. They saw a most irregular, harrowing outcome.

Instead of Brady, man of many memorable comebacks, it was Wilson who launched his team. After a turgid start, he delivered the performance of his abbreviated pro career, staggering the Pats.

"The lift—you could see it in our players—as we were finishing the game was really something to make you proud as a coach," said coach Pete Carroll, whose four-speed oral transmission found a fifth gear. "It took every play, every kick, every rush—everything we did had to happen like it did for us to have a chance.

"I just loved the way we rallied on both sides of the ball and special teams, knowing that we had a chance to win. It's a big statement for this young team—more so because (of New England and) the championship ways they know.

"Russell played a fantastic game."

For five weeks, impatient Seahawks fans waited for the expectations heaped upon Wilson by Carroll to pay off on the decision to start him over Matt Flynn. Wilson delivered.

Free of fumbles and interceptions that hurt him earlier in the season, and sacked only twice behind improved protection, Wilson had a quarterback rating of 133.7, hitting on 16-of-27 passes for a career-high 293 yards and three touchdowns (Brady's rating was 79.3).

He led fourth-quarter touchdown drives of 83 and 57 yards, the latter concluding with a 46-yard strike to a wide-open Sidney Rice at the goal line with 1:18 remaining. The touchdown, followed by Steven Hauschka's decisive extra

Russell Wilson threw three touchdowns and delivered a 133.1 passer rating against the New England Patriots October 14, 2012. (Photo by Drew McKenzie)

point, sent ripples of energy through the stadium that tectonically resembled the Beast Quake of the 2010 playoffs.

"He really had his eyes down the field on that," Carroll said of Wilson. "It was a fantastic play."

"I was in awe, man. In awe," said cornerback Richard Sherman of Wilson on the final drive. "He was a magician, he was magnificent. That's the reason he was starting. A lot of people have doubted him. He shut 'em all down today. He beat Tom Brady, he beat Aaron Rodgers (Green Bay), he beat Tony Romo (Dallas). Not a lot of rookies do that."

Sherman forgot about Wilson beating Cam Newton (Carolina) in Week 5. Sherman also wouldn't have known it, but this was true: Six games into Wilson's NFL career, he defeated two quarterbacks—Brady (XXXVI, XXXVIII, XXXIX) and Rodgers (XLV)—with Super Bowl rings.

Before Wilson, and dating to the 1970 NFL-AFL merger, only five rookie quarterbacks bested two Super Bowl-winning quarterbacks. Joe Ferguson of Buffalo defeated Len Dawson of Kansas City and Joe Namath of the New York Jets in 1973; Steve Fuller of Kansas City defeated Ken Stabler of Oakland twice in 1979; Mark Sanchez of the Jets knocked off Brady and Peyton Manning in 2009; and Colt McCoy of Cleveland beat Brady and Drew Brees in 2010.

Now here was Wilson, all 5'10 $^5/_8$" of him, toppling giants.

Another Wilson nugget in what would eventually become a gold mine by the end of his rookie season: Wilson's game-winner to Rice, which traveled 57 yards in the air, marked the longest by a rookie inside the two-minute warning since 1999, when Tim Couch threw a 56-yarder on the final play to give Cleveland a 21–16 win at New Orleans.

Wilson, who jacked his passer rating from 75.6 to 85.6 against the Patriots, moved into second place among the five rookie quarterbacks who had their debuts in 2012. All but Wilson went in the first round of the NFL draft. ■

Above: Safety Earl Thomas returns a Tom Brady interception 23 yards during Seattle's 24–23 come-from-behind victory over the New England Patriots. Opposite: Russell Wilson threw for a then-career high 293 yards and three touchdowns in Seattle's 24–23 comeback victory over New England October 14, 2012. (Photos by Drew McKenzie)

NOTHING LIKE IT IN 63 YEARS

Three-Game Offensive Streak Tatters NFL Record Books

Panned for drafting Russell Wilson, general manager John Schneider and head coach Pete Carroll were suddenly coming in for universal praise for making what one SI.com columnist called "a visionary pick." Carroll didn't trust Wilson yet with the entire playbook, but the Seahawks were 4–4 at the halfway point, not that far away from 8–0, but not that far away, truth be told, from 1–7.

Over the next three weeks, the Seahawks went 3–1, beating the Minnesota Vikings (30–20), the New York Jets (28–7), and the Chicago Bears (23–17), while losing only at Miami (24–21). In those four games, Wilson tossed nine touchdown passes, no interceptions, posted four consecutive 100.0-plus passer ratings, and showed a different aspect to his game every week.

On Seattle's second possession against Minnesota, second-and-five at Seattle's 27-yard line, Wilson play-faked from the shotgun and completed a 23-yard screamer snagged by Sidney Rice—and would have struck out Albert Pujols, looking. It permanently silenced anyone who said Wilson lacked the arm strength to play in the NFL.

A week later, against the Jets, Wilson began showing off his legs, accumulating a career-high 34 yards, including 18 on a read option play, newly introduced into the Seattle offense. In the loss to Miami, when the Seahawks didn't get a first down for the first 16 minutes and the defense gave up 17 points in the final eight, Wilson proved he could overcome misplays by his teammates and miscalls by his coaches. He completed 22-of-27 passes, including 16 in a row, an NFL rookie record.

If one game is identified as the moment Wilson shed his apprenticeship, and after which was granted full access to the playbook, it was the breathtaking 23–17 overtime triumph over the Chicago Bears at Soldier Field on December 2, four days after Wilson's 24th birthday.

That day, Wilson had to win the game twice. So he did, taking the Seahawks 97 yards at the end of regulation for the game-tying touchdown and 80 yards in overtime for the winning score.

To force OT, Wilson twice overcame second-and-10, successfully negotiated third-and-14, and then converted fourth-and-3 from the Chicago 48. To get into position to throw the game-winning, overtime touchdown to Rice, Wilson converted third-and-2 from the Chicago 47 (he skirted left end for five yards), third-and-5 from the 37 (ran for 12 yards), and third-and-10 from the 25 (13-yard pass to Doug Baldwin).

"It was great execution by the quarterback," said a beaming Pete Carroll. "He used the play calls properly, and took advantage of the things he saw. I think we all realize now the guy we have playing quarterback for us is amazing."

Or as cornerback Richard Sherman put it, "He's one

At Chicago on December 2, 2012, Russell Wilson directed length-of-the-field drives at the end of regulation and in overtime to give the Seahawks a 23–17 victory. (Photo by Drew McKenzie)

team. He believes in his preparation. And he prepares like no other. The kid gives us a chance every game."

Something clicked for Wilson, selected NFC Offensive Player of the Week for his performance against the Bears. Something also clicked for the Seahawks, who followed with the greatest three-game scoring binge in franchise history: 58–0 over Arizona (even Matt Flynn played), 50–17 over Buffalo in Toronto, and 42–13 over San Francisco in a nationally televised Sunday night game at the Clink.

In the Buffalo rout, Wilson became the first quarterback in Seattle history to rush for three touchdowns in a game, scoring on strolls of 14, 25, and 13 yards. He also became the first NFL quarterback to rush for three touchdowns in a game since Daunte Culpepper of Minnesota against Chicago on September 3, 2000. Scoring once on a scramble out of the pocket and twice on read options, Wilson finished with a career-high 92 rushing yards (franchise record for a quarterback). More impressive than his yardage total, the Bills did not tackle Wilson once.

By scoring 50 points against Buffalo one week after squashing Arizona with 58, the Seahawks became the first team since the 1950 Los Angeles Rams and New York Giants to tally 50 or more in back-to-back weeks.

After the Seahawks followed those outbursts with the pasting of the rival 49ers (only the 1950 Rams scored more in a three-week span), Wilson hit another personal milestone—his first pro game with four touchdown passes. Carroll was quizzed for the umpteenth time about the development of his quarterback. He didn't hesitate.

"He's got it nailed." ■

of the best in the league, rookie or not. At the end of the game, he drove down the field against that defense like nothing was on him. Great quarterback."

As evidenced by 23 completions in 37 attempts, two touchdown passes, no turnovers, and an even more crucial 71 yards on nine carries, Wilson advanced past the most optimistic preseason projections for him.

When the Seahawks' defense let down in the final 15 seconds and allowed the Bears to tie the game at 17 on a Robbie Gould field goal on the final play of regulation, Wilson repeated the feat of a field-length drive against a defense that led the NFL in takeaways. Winning the coin toss, the Seahawks took the ball and re-won the contest without the Bears touching the ball. It wasn't easy, but it was nearly flawless, thanks in part to the read option made for Wilson's running skills.

"He is amazing," fullback Michael Robinson said. "He keeps believing. He believes in himself. He believes in this

Above: Seahawks coach Pete Carroll and general manager John Schneider performed a total remake of the team's roster after they joined the franchise in 2010. At Schneider's urging, the Seahawks selected quarterback Russell Wilson in the 2012 NFL Draft. (Photo by Drew McKenzie) Opposite: Cornerback Richard Sherman makes his fourth interception of the 2012 season, picking off Mark Sanchez in the fourth quarter of the Seahawks' 28–7 win over the Jets. (Photo by Drew Sellers)

ROOKIE IN THE POSTSEASON

Wilson Leads Seahawks to First Playoff Road Win in 30 Years

The Seahawks finished the 2012 regular season 11–5 after a 20–13 comeback win over the St. Louis Rams. Despite taking six sacks and absorbing seven quarterback hits, Russell Wilson recorded his highest passer rating—136.3—and ninth of 100.0-plus, a single-season franchise record. Of more importance, Wilson made a defining decision—one that underscored Pete Carroll's remark "He's got it nailed"—with the score tied at 13 inside two minutes.

Wilson faced a first-and-goal quandary at the St. Louis one-yard line: Attempt to run from the pocket for a score, or attempt throw a pass and break the single-season touchdown rookie record set by NFL demi-god Peyton Manning? After a second of pondering a blast of individual glory, Wilson ran the ball.

"I realized," he said of pursuing the passing record, "that's not me."

"Not a single soul on this earth could have imagined he would have done that this season," said wide receiver Golden Tate of matching Manning.

Content with a co-record, Wilson went untouched to a corner pylon. The score ushered the Seahawks into the postseason against the 10–6 Washington Redskins and the most celebrated read-option quarterback in the league, rookie Robert Griffin III, the No. 2 overall pick in the 2012 NFL draft. The development begged for a larger perspective on quarterbacks.

The Redskins nearly sold the Washington Monument to move up in that draft to get Griffin. The Colts, slavering for Stanford's Andrew Luck, were willing in 2011 to Suck for Luck—a 3–13 season. And Denver boss John Elway ignored the risk inherent in Manning's much-repaired, 36-year-old body, as well as the $96 million deal over five years required to hire it.

The Seahawks? They expended a third-round draft choice on Wilson, stood firm in the harshness of mockery, and reaped the same reward as those who spent huge treasure. And the Seahawks, as well as the rest of the NFL, were merely on the outer edge of understanding the significance of Wilson's hire by Seattle.

Sports history can turn on a single play, as Mariners icon Edgar Martinez continues to remind Seattle every time a replay of his franchise-altering, 1995 double into the left-field corner against the Yankees is replayed—still to appreciative cheers after two decades. History also can pivot on a misplay. But at the moment of a messed-up handoff between Wilson and Marshawn Lynch in the second quarter of the Seahawks' wild card playoff game at Washington on January 6, 2013, it only seemed to make a 14-0 deficit look more grim.

But no.

Russell Wilson produced an 11–5 won-lost regular-season record as a starting quarterback in 2012 and was named *Sports Illustrated's* Offensive Rookie of the Year. (Photo by Drew McKenzie)

Or as Pete Carroll put it, "They were kicking our butts, no doubt about that. Then they didn't."

On first-and-five at the Seattle 45, Wilson and Lynch botched the handoff on a read option, a common outcome of the play in the college game that helped keep the trickery out of pro football. But this time, Lynch bailed out the Seahawks with a play that ranks among the great rescues in club history. As the ball squibbed along the ground, Lynch alertly peeled back and, instead of pouncing, kept his feet, scooped up the ball and blew past the disorganized Washington defense for a 20-yard gain. That led to Seattle's first touchdown. The climb from the hole was underway.

The climb was aided by the dubious decision of Washington coach Mike Shanahan to allow Griffin to play on a sore knee that troubled him much of the season, even though Washington arrived on the playoffs on a seven-game

win streak. Griffin was finally pulled in the fourth quarter, long after the expiration of his efficiency.

The Seahawks, meanwhile, were going the other way—gaining strength by the minute despite the hectoring from the largest crowd (84,325) in Redskins history.

Steady as a dial tone, Wilson led the Seahawks to 24 unanswered points and something unseen by Seattle sports fans in 30 years—a Seahawks playoff win on the NFL road.

The triumph broke a string of nine consecutive road losses in the postseason dating to December 31, 1983, when Steve Largent was in his heyday. The win also made the Seahawks the third team, following the 1957 Detroit Lions and 2003 Philadelphia Eagles, to win a playoff game after being down 14 points to start.

In his first NFL playoff game, Wilson completed 15-of-26 passes for 187 yards, one touchdown, and no interceptions for a passer rating of 92.9. But his running was almost as important. Against the NFL's No. 5 rushing defense, Wilson scrambled for 67 yards on eight carries, for 8.4 yards per attempt. That helped keep Seattle's young defenders, who surrendered only 24 yards of offense over the final three periods, off the field.

"It is a little weird," said Seahawks fullback Michael Robinson of Wilson. "To keep his composure in this wild environment, first playoff game for him and all…it's just weird. But Russell Wilson always does it. I've seen veteran, older quarterbacks crumble and crack in the same situation. Not him." ∎

Above: Russell Wilson scores on a one-yard run in Seattle's 20–13 victory over the St. Louis Rams December 30, 2012, at CenturyLink Field. Wilson ran for 58 yards on 10 carries. Opposite: Marshawn Lynch, taking a handoff from Russell Wilson, produced 11 100-yard rushing games, including playoffs, in 2012. Overall, he ran for 1,590 yards and 11 touchdowns. (Photos by Drew McKenzie)

CHAPTER 4

ASSEMBLING THE PARTS

Russell Wilson watches the clock run down at the end of the Seahawks' 30–28 loss to Atlanta in the NFC divisional playoffs on January 13, 2013. (Photo by Drew McKenzie)

SUBLIME MATCH

Seahawks Leadership Clicks with Carroll, Schneider, Wilson

In the aftermath of Seattle's 30–28 loss to the Atlanta Falcons in the NFC divisional playoff game at the Georgia Dome, despair overwhelmed the Seahawks locker room. Players struggled to come to grips with a major opportunity lost. Richard Sherman, the verbose cornerback seemingly fated to die in mid-sentence, waved off reporters. Safety Earl Thomas shook his head no to questions.

So it went until, finally, tight end Zach Miller, buoyed by the individual game of his career (eight catches, 142 yards, one glorious touchdown), had the presence of mind to drill down past the anguish to the core of the ache.

"We wanted to win it," Miller said, "for him."

Miller referred to Russell Wilson, the kid as relentless as Puget Sound rain, who had spent the majority of his rookie season bumping into history and ended it by nearly standing it on its head.

Wilson brought the Seahawks screaming back from a 20–0 halftime deficit for a 28–27 lead with 34 seconds left, leaving ashen the red-clad hordes in the Georgia Dome. But they erupted anew when Matt Bryant drilled a 49-yard field goal with eight seconds left to win the game. The Seahawks foolishly played a soft zone that allowed quarterback Matt Ryan two long completions that set up Bryant's kick.

The whipsaw brought a devastating end to Wilson's brilliant rookie season. But Wilson refused to mope, demonstrating why the team had fallen for a rookie it came to cherish.

"When the game was over, I was very disappointed, but when I got to the tunnel, walking off, I got so excited for the opportunity next year I couldn't wait to get into the off-season and work and work and work to get the Seahawks into the Super Bowl," said Wilson, who had a metaphorical arrow shot through his heart and already pulled it out.

Later, on the team bus, Wilson approached coach Pete Carroll and shared his vision. What Wilson didn't know was that Carroll, even after the devastating defeat, felt the same way.

"That's what I was thinking," Carroll said. "Let's not just win one Super Bowl. Let's win several."

Events would prove the epiphany the men shared on the bus ride to the Atlanta airport would play out in 2013 just as they saw it. After one NFL season, it was apparent that Wilson was Carroll's nearly perfect quarterback, and Carroll was Wilson's nearly perfect coach. That combination is the Holy Grail in the NFL. To appreciate how even more unlikely its occurrence was in Seattle requires a glance back at the Seahawks' pre-Carroll history. It makes the Wilson success story look almost predictable.

Four years after the Seahawks' first championship appearance, Super Bowl XL in Detroit following the 2005 season, the franchise was, competitively speaking, nearly dead. Coach Mike Holmgren's final year of 2008 was a 4–12 dud. After a 4–7 start in 2009, general manager Tim Ruskell was fired. That season ended 5–11 after losses in

Change hyphen to em dash and fix date so it reads: Russell Wilson exchanges handshakes with Atlanta players following Seattle's 30–28 divisional playoff loss to the Falcons in the Georgia Dome on January 13, 2013. (Photo by Drew McKenzie)

the final four games by a combined score of 123–37. The closing debacle prompted the shocking firing of Holmgren's successor, hometown favorite Jim Mora, after a single season.

After reaching the pinnacle in 2006, the Seahawks were a weak third in a weak NFC West, had no GM, and were searching for their third coach in three years. Yet from that compost pile bloomed a revival.

Carroll, at the time presiding over a mighty USC program dominating college ball, did not have advance understanding of the gravity of NCAA sanctions that were about to hit his employer over cash payments made years earlier by a representative of an agent to the family of star Trojans running back Reggie Bush. Carroll and athletic director Mike Garrett were certain the worst it would be was some scholarship losses. They were planning around it for the following season.

Then the Seahawks called Carroll. A long shot to hire a big shot.

"He was," as one Seahawks staffer put it, "the king of Los Angeles."

After being fired from the Jets after a year (6–10, 1994), and after three years in New England (27–21, 1997–99), Carroll was chastened by his experience in the NFL, yet never dismissive of another chance. It had to be a fit where he had authority to do it his way.

His astounding success at USC—seven Pac-10 titles in a row and two national championships (2003–04)—kept him sufficiently secure that he turned down several inquiries from NFL teams until he heard what he wanted to hear to make his vision work: Control over decision-making on personnel.

Carroll never forgot the March 1998 loss of five-time All-Pro running back Curtis Martin after Carroll's first year with the Patriots. The eventual Pro Football Hall of Famer left in free agency to the division-rival Jets in a six-year, $36 million deal.

"That was my best player," Carroll told people at the time, bewildered, figuring the Pats could have found a way to keep a game-changing talent.

In Seattle in 2009, things were falling apart. Mora,

a voluble sort who once talked his way out of the head coaching job with the NFL Atlanta Falcons, was at it again.

Particularly after the third game, when he criticized kicker Olindo Mare for missing two field goals in a 29–25 home loss to Chicago.

"There's no excuses for those," Mora said angrily postgame. "If you're a kicker in the NFL you should make those kicks—bottom line. End of story. Period. No excuses. No wind, doesn't matter. You've gotta makes those kicks…It's not acceptable. Not acceptable. Absolutely not acceptable."

In the NFL and all team sports, that kind of public candor is deemed unwise because of its impacts on players' attitudes. Mora should have known better, but he had always been a man of impulse. He began to lose his locker room.

The fade reached its nadir in a December 20 home game against 1–12 Tampa Bay, which beat listless Seattle 24–7. Club president Tod Leiweke, who agreed to hire Mora at the recommendation of Ruskell, was as furious as he was fearful. His worry: The fabled 12th Man, symbol of Seattle's fervent home fans created in the Kingdome days of the early 1980s, would slip away.

But if the embarrassing home loss to the Bucs put Leiweke over the edge regarding Mora, it also put him in a jam. Not only had Leiweke strongly endorsed Mora at the time of Ruskell's departure, the selection of a coaching successor normally fell to the general manager. But after firing Ruskell, Seattle had no general manager.

That imminent debacle would prove fortuitous. At the time, that wasn't possible to see.

"We were really in trouble," a Seahawks front-office staffer said. "We needed a big idea."

Or as Leiweke later called it in an email, "a 360-degree idea"—a hire that not only would get attention, but create a connection beyond the winning of games.

The coaching hire took precedence over the general manager search, which had quietly been underway since mid-season. It was apparent that the talent judgments of Ruskell, a longtime scout who in his first Seattle year of 2005 helped get the Seahawks to the franchise's first Super Bowl appearance, weren't working. Plus, he handled awkwardly the public chores of the job, then asked for a

contract extension that Leiweke was unwilling to provide.

Leiweke, hired in 2003, had long career experience in pro sports and connecting with fans, and was well-connected within the industry. He created a short list of general manager candidates, then put it aside to start a fresh list for a coaching search. Former NFL head coaches Tony Dungy and Bill Cowher were briefly considered, but Leiweke wanted something more.

He wanted Pete Carroll.

The Trojans finished what was, for them, a down year at 9–4, 5–4 in the Pac-10 Conference that included a 16–13 loss at Husky Stadium to Washington and new coach Steve Sarkisian, Carroll's former offensive coordinator.

Contact through Carroll's agent was made, but nothing would happen until after December 26, when USC beat Boston College in the Emerald Bowl in San Francisco. The next day, the Seahawks lost in Green Bay 48–10, and a week later closed the season with a 17–13 home loss to Tennessee.

The faster Mora sank, the more Carroll rose. Not only did Carroll have a winning record (33–31) in the NFL, someone looked at Carroll's bowl game/non-conference record and discovered it was 34–1, the only loss to Texas in the 2005 national title game. Big games and thorough preparation appeared to be the Carroll house specialty.

Leiweke also was taken by the impact of "A Better LA," Carroll's nonprofit organization he founded that supported community-based solutions to restore peace in inner-city Los Angeles.

"Tod said, 'The premise was crazy,'" said someone who was with Leiweke in early January 2010. "Taking guys in the 'hood, turning them into mentors, and letting them go save lives.' The truth was, it worked."

Carroll, too, gathered information about the Seahawks and Seattle, and liked what he found. The San Francisco native always preferred the West Coast. Paul Allen, the NFL's wealthiest owner, certainly had the resources, and

The Seahawks hired Pete Carroll on January 10, 2010, and days later, working from a club-compiled list, Carroll hired John Schneider as the team's general manager. Almost immediately, the pair embarked upon a complete roster remake. (Photo by Drew Sellers)

paid $80 million for a top-tier headquarters building/practice facility in a Seattle suburb. Once apprised of the Mora mistake, Allen also didn't blink at paying Mora the $16 million owed him on the balance of his coaching contract.

Most important, Carroll was proposed to be the football boss. In Seattle at the moment, there was neither a general manager nor a meddlesome owner. When it came to football, Allen was hands-off, the anti-Jerry Jones.

So Carroll agreed to talk. Leiweke and Seahawks general counsel Lance Lopes, who had been with the Seahawks since 2001, flew to Los Angeles with Bert Kolde, Allen's longtime personal friend and a member of the Seahawks board of directors. They met Carroll and his agent at a private home for dinner.

Leiweke and Lopes were already persuaded, but Kolde would be the one to advise Allen.

By the end of dinner, Carroll and Kolde liked what they heard from each other. Carroll asked for some time, and flew to Hawaii to discuss it with family. He agreed to talk with Allen by phone. Afterward came the call to Leiweke: "I'm in."

But to get the five-year, $33 million contract, Carroll had to agree to a stipulation: He had control over football operations, including the choice of general manager, but he had to choose from the list of four that Leiweke created in the search for Ruskell's successor, then set aside.

The Seahawks' apprehension came largely from the full control that Holmgren was given when he was hired away from Green Bay in 1999, then had his general manager duties stripped away four years later when the multi-hatted "Big Show" wasn't working. The latter decision helped get the Seahawks to their first Super Bowl.

This time, the Seahawks were willing to give Carroll some choice, but not from among his football friends. As one Seahawks front office official put it, "Sometimes, you have to protect these guys from themselves."

The Seahawks hired Carroll on January 10, 2010. Nine days later he hired Schneider, a total stranger and a generation younger, who spent eight seasons learning football's wise ways in Green Bay.

The oddness of a coach hiring what would normally be his boss was described by the club as "a collaboration," a much-derided term in local media. So was the whole situation in Seattle, where many fans resented Carroll for his USC success, and Schneider was a low-profile, 39-year-old vagabond (five NFL teams, including 2000 in Seattle) unknown even to Carroll.

Plus, there were two high-profile local casualties.

Mora, a former University of Washington player and graduate assistant coach, a one-time hot property who was also a popular choice for the Washington Huskies' vacancy filled by Sarkisian, was out on the sidewalk.

Then there was Holmgren, eager to come out of semi-retirement to be the club president. He nearly got the job, but when the money and control weren't what he wanted, he took a better offer from the Cleveland Browns—but not before suggesting publicly that the Seahawks were in disarray. That didn't go over well in Renton.

After the two unusual hires of January 2010, no Seahawks follower was encouraged, much less fantasizing about Super Bowls. But in the first year, Carroll and Schneider coaxed a playoff appearance out of a 7–9 team—the first in NFL history to make the postseason with a losing record. They even beat in the playoffs the defending Super Bowl champion New Orleans Saints, a delirious outcome in which the "Beast Quake" touchdown run by Marshawn Lynch introduced the sports world to the seismic influence of the 12th Man.

But after a second 7–9 season (no playoffs), doubts remained. It took until the remarkable three-game run of 150 points for Seattle fans, and later the rest of the NFL, to see the potent potential in the original path taken by Carroll as a teacher and leader, as well as the talent evaluations from the collaboration between Carroll and Schneider.

Ultimate success awaited, but it would not have happened without the precocious, inexpensive Wilson at quarterback. And Wilson as rookie starter would not have happened without Carroll in Seattle and Schneider at his side, working from the ashes. And without the wrenching loss in Atlanta that left humbled and speechless a loquacious, bodacious bunch of football swashbucklers, the acute intensity of 2013 may not have come to be. ∎

Russell Wilson led the Seahawks back from a 20-point deficit in the 2012 NFC divisional playoffs, only to watch Seattle lose to Atlanta on a late field goal. (Photo by Drew McKenzie)

BASE CAMP ESTABLISHED; SUMMIT AHEAD

Seahawks Build to a Championship

After Russell Wilson concluded an historic rookie season by throwing three touchdowns in the NFC's 62–35 victory over the AFC in the Pro Bowl (his 147.1 pass rating was best among the all-star game's quarterbacks), he was nominated for several awards, including NFL Offensive Rookie of the Year, an ESPY for "Breakthrough Athlete of the Year," and the Pepsi Max Rookie of the Year.

Although Wilson won only the Pepsi Max trophy, the fact that he was in line for any postseason honor underscored the progress he'd made between the time the Seahawks selected him in the 2012 draft and his near-record upset of the Falcons in the NFC divisional playoffs.

Wilson's height, which compromised his draft stock, was not a problem. He figured out early how to find or create throwing lanes. According to his coaches and teammates, his work ethic, leadership, and intangibles had been off the charts. So were some of his numbers.

Wilson tied Peyton Manning's 1998 record for most touchdown passes by a rookie (26); threw a game-winning touchdown in the final two minutes of regulation or overtime three times, most by a rookie since the 1970 merger; set a rookie record with three consecutive games—vs. Minnesota (November 4), vs. New York Jets (November 11), at Miami (November 25)—with a 125.0 passer rating or better; and became the first player in history to record three rushing touchdowns and pass for another in the first half of a game (December 16 at Buffalo).

Wilson's second-year challenge, which also held true for Andrew Luck and Robert Griffin III, would center around his ability to make adjustments after defenses threw new wrinkles at him.

Wilson also succeeded in making Matt Flynn expendable. On April 1, 2013, unwilling to pay a backup more than five times as much as the starter, and with a savings of $5.25 million in cash and $3.25 million in cap space, the Seahawks traded Flynn to Oakland. Entirely expected since Flynn had barely seen the field, the swap was one of two Seattle made prior to the 2013 draft.

So confident were the Seahawks in their personnel build-out that they dealt their top pick, 25th overall, to Minnesota, part of the price to acquire wide receiver/kick returner/prime-time gamebreaker Percy Harvin. That meant that the Seahawks, Carroll in particular, determined that their future was right bloody now.

Within hours of Harvin's introduction to Seattle media,

Russell Wilson recorded a pair of victories over Super Bowl-winning quarterbacks in 2012, beating Tom Brady of New England and Aaron Rodgers of Green Bay. (Photo by Drew McKenzie)

Jim Harbaugh and the 49ers announced the signing of wide receiver Anquan Boldin, a free agent from Baltimore. The Seahawks and 49ers would meet September 15 at the Clink and again on December 8 in the Bay Area, two games circled as must-see division deciders.

After adding Harvin to the offense, the Seahawks moved to buttress a defense that held opponents to a league-low 15.3 points, but had a variety of issues, none good.

Defensive end Chris Clemons, the team's sacks leader (11.5), suffered a torn ACL during Seattle's wild card victory over the Redskins. The Seahawks did not know when he would return. As soon as free agency opened, the Seahawks signed defensive end Cliff Avril from Detroit to a two-year deal; 6'7", 295-pound defensive tackle Tony McDaniel from Miami; and defensive end Michael Bennett from Tampa Bay, who had a cup of coffee with the Seahawks as an undrafted free agent in 2009, on a one-year, $5 million deal.

Those signings became more significant when, on May 17, defensive end Bruce Irvin, taken in the first round of the same draft that netted Wilson, received a four-game suspension for use of performance enhancing drugs. That continued a pattern of foolishness by several Seahawks players, including cornerback Brandon Browner, banished for four games near the end of the 2012 regular season.

Without condoning his misbehavior, the Seahawks stood publicly behind Browner. They did not do the same with starting linebacker LeRoy Hill after his career arrest total reached four (vs. 1.5 sacks), or with backup quarterback Josh Portis, released after a DUI arrest.

Carroll brought in several veterans to audition as Wilson's backup, including Matt Leinart, who won the 2004 Heisman Trophy at USC when Carroll coached the Trojans; Cleveland castoff Brady Quinn; former Seahawks backup Seneca Wallace; and Tyler Thigpen, another career backup. But Carroll finally settled on Tarvaris Jackson, the first loser in the Wilson-Flynn-Jackson "open competition," brought back after his release by the Bills.

Carroll had his first look at the second-year Wilson June 12 during a mandatory three-day mini-camp at the VMAC practice field. After watching Wilson sling bullets, Carroll had a hard time keeping his industrial-grade optimism in check.

"He's so much further ahead than he was last year at this time," Carroll said. "He's in such greater command. Just imagine—this was the first mini-camp with the vets for him last year. It's amazing how far he's come."

Before it was asked, Carroll posed the question himself: How could Wilson possibly top what he did in 2012?

"It would be hard for anybody to come back and have a better year," Carroll said. "But he's worked hard to command every aspect of what the quarterback position calls for—at the line of scrimmage, coming out of the huddle, pre-snap alerts, line of scrimmage calls, protections and run calls, the whole thing. We've given him everything, and he's worked to refine it and get it nailed. I couldn't ask for more in terms of his preparation than what he's putting together."

"I think the biggest thing is just focusing on the day, the next couple hours," Wilson said. "Stay in the moment. Stay in the now. Whenever I do that, I have a better opportunity to play at a high level."

"He's going straight ahead," said Carroll. "He's going to keep balling."

More than any other factor, that was why the Seahawks were becoming a team on the verge of its dreams catching up with its prowess. ▪

Russell Wilson won three major awards following his rookie season, including selection to the NFL Pro Bowl, Pepsi Max Rookie of the Year, and *Sports Illustrated* Offensive Rookie of the Year. (Photo by Drew McKenzie)

CHAPTER 5

BOOK OF PETE

A two-time national college champion at USC, Pete Carroll brought a different style to the NFL, one numerous skeptics said would fail. But he believed in his system and had the perfect place to try it out—Seattle. (Photo by Drew Sellers)

MANAGING THE PRESEASON HYPE

Pundits Peg Seahawks as Super Bowl Favorites

Despite a 30–28 divisional playoff loss to the Atlanta Falcons, the Seahawks made such a positive impression during the 2012 postseason run that national media designated them the "It Team For '13," as one magazine put it. Russell Wilson and cornerback Richard Sherman appeared on the cover of *Sports Illustrated*. Wilson also made the cover of *ESPN The Magazine's* NFL preview issue, the headline blaring, "Pumped For a Super Season."

Although many pundits and oddsmakers picked the Seahawks to reach Super Bowl XLVIII, that didn't guarantee a thing, especially given the gauntlet the Seahawks would have to face in the NFC West. San Francisco was coming off a Super Bowl appearance, and Arizona and St. Louis both presented Seattle serious defensive matchup problems.

The Seahawks also faced a treacherous start. Their first five opponents included three 2012 playoff teams—49ers, Texans, Colts—and three of the first five games would be played on the road, at Carolina, Houston, and Indianapolis. A 1–4 start, with only Jacksonville at home a gimme, seemed possible if the Seahawks stumbled in any way.

Although the preseason attention accorded Wilson and Seahawks mainly served to grease the vast NFL hype machine, it also validated what 62-year-old Pete Carroll accomplished in his three years as Seattle's head coach.

Hired January 10, 2010, following a fabulous career at USC, where he won seven Pac-10 championships and a BCS title, Carroll weathered stiff criticism following his appointment. He was ridiculed for bailing on the Trojans just ahead of an advancing NCAA posse that would sanction USC for a variety of infractions and was also panned for his previous shortcomings as an NFL head man.

His stints as head coach the New York Jets (1994) and New England Patriots (1997–99) ended with invitations to try his luck elsewhere. In many ways he had been fortunate to land at USC, where he had not been the first choice to replace Paul Hackett. But as Carroll successfully rebuilt his reputation with the Trojans as a coach who liked to engage emotionally his players, he wondered how he would do things differently if he received another NFL shot.

Carroll received part of the answer from former USC players who returned to the Los Angeles campus disillusioned with their experiences in the NFL, particularly the hard-assed, often dehumanizing approach many teams took in conducting team business, particularly with respect to player relations.

Carroll had a natural rainbows and lollipops personality and came to believe there was a different way to win—principally with high-octane energy and enthusiasm while treating players as valued employees rather than replaceable

Coach Pete Carroll and GM John Schneider uncovered gems in and out of the NFL draft. They signed wide receiver Doug Baldwin, a Stanford graduate, as a rookie free agent in 2011. He led the Seahawks in receiving with 51 catches his first year in the league. (Photo by Drew McKenzie)

commodities. But when the Seahawks gave Carroll a chance to test his approach, skeptics declared that style would never work in the NFL.

What the public mainly saw during Carroll's first two years in Seattle was the astonishing roster churn, 284 transactions in 2010 and more than 500 by the end of 2011. By the end of 2012, when 10-year cornerback Marcus Trufant finally left, not a single player remained from Seattle's Super Bowl XL team. By the time Carroll set his roster for 2013, he and Schneider had made more than 1,000 player transactions —numerous players coming and going before they ever saw the field—in order to get to the 53 men they thought could win a Super Bowl.

What neither public nor press could have known: Carroll and Schneider were not merely sorting through tons of high-priced talent. They were looking for and signing players who possessed specific physical gifts and skills as well as a receptivity to intense position competition and the personal empowerment Carroll provided.

For all the millions he made coaching football, Carroll could have tripled his income as a corporate motivational speaker. It was not only what he said, but how he said it. Carroll rarely had need for punctuation marks—he typically put periods on the waiver wire—in his fast-paced soliloquies.

Carroll encouraged the Seahawks in a variety of ways. He blared music during practice, supported basketball and bowling competitions among his players, and introduced them to yoga and meditation exercises. Carroll delivered simple, consistent messages. Above all: "Always compete," the root of Wilson's platitudes in almost every press conference. In Russellspeak, every week was championship week, every game a championship opportunity.

Not all Seahawks bought into Carroll. One who didn't was Matt Flynn, who lost his job to Wilson during 2012 training camp. After the Seahawks traded Flynn to Oakland a year later, Flynn knocked Carroll's philosophy on his way out of Seattle, telling *The Los Angeles Times* he didn't have the personality of a "hoo-rah guy."

Wilson was the perfect Carroll player. He bought into yoga and mediation, developed mantras of his own, and had a keen interest in the nature of success, one of Carroll's favorite topics.

When Wilson attended ESPN's ESPY Awards show in Los Angeles prior to the opening of training camp, he sought out LeBron James, Dwyane Wade, and Chris Bosh of the Miami Heat, coming off a second consecutive NBA title.

Wilson specifically wanted to know how they maintained their success. He came away with an answer that failed to include any mention of the obvious reason: talent.

"They basically said was that it comes down to hard work and discipline," Wilson told *ESPN The Magazine*. "But also the camaraderie they had was unbelievable."

Two days before the Seahawks wrapped up a 4–0 preseason with a 22–6 victory over the Oakland Raiders, Carroll invited Heat head coach Erik Spoelstra to visit the VMAC and speak to the Seahawks about how to cope with unprecedented preseason expectations and suffocating national media attention. Spoelstra addressed several topics, including "absorbing hype" and "deflecting criticism," keys, in his view, to making a deep playoff run.

Reporters did not hear directly from Spoelstra, a Portland, Oregon, native who attended Jesuit High in Beaverton before a successful college basketball career at the University of Portland, but Wilson spoke for him after the session.

"The sacrifice that it takes to be great and to be great so often is what he was talking about," Wilson said. "Just to be around him, spend that time with him, and break down the success that they've had, why they've had it, and why they've had it so often—that was the best part about it.

Pete Carroll and his coaching staff installed the read option in order to take advantage of Russell Wilson's amazing mobility. Wilson responded with 489 rushing yards and four touchdowns as a rookie. (Photo by Drew McKenzie)

"I think the biggest thing that correlates with us and the Miami Heat is the way we practice and the way we go about our business. We can't compare ourselves to them yet. We haven't done anything. They've done a great job of winning the whole thing. That's what we want to learn from them. For Coach Carroll and Coach Spoelstra to be able to get together and share words and sift thoughts, that will be a huge advantage for us.

"Just working hard, continuing to believe, and ignoring the noise. That's the main message Coach Spoelstra gave, and it clicked with us."

The Seahawks did not become one of the favorites to win Super Bowl XLVIII because they could breathe in, breathe out, and tap into their chakras better than the 49ers or Green Bay Packers. Carroll and Schneider had constructed a deep, versatile roster of quality talent. Even after it absorbed three major hits, national expectations still ran high.

First was Chris Clemons' torn ACL against Washington in the 2012 wild-card game. Carroll couldn't predict when exactly Clemons would play, much less return to form. Bruce Irvin's PED suspension came next. He would miss the first four games, including three against strong playoff contenders: Carolina (September 8), San Francisco (September 15), and Houston (September 29).

Percy Harvin, who cost the Seahawks three draft picks and $25.5 million in guaranteed money in a trade with Minnesota, came up lame the first week of training camp with a torn hip labrum, creating endless radio talk show fodder about whether he was a need or a luxury and whether the Seahawks could win a Super Bowl without him. By the end of camp, Harvin had surgery and wouldn't return until November.

None of the absences squelched Super Bowl talk in Seattle, which only ratcheted up as the Seahawks raced through a perfect preseason.

Wilson played only two series in a 31–10 victory at San Diego as Carroll gave the rest of the snaps to Wilson's auditioning backups, Tarvaris Jackson and Brady Quinn. Matched against Peyton Manning and the Denver Broncos in the second preseason game, Wilson threw for 127 yards and two touchdowns in two quarters to Manning's 163 yards and one in a quarter and a half.

Neither Wilson nor Manning was the story of the night. Looking to secure a roster spot with Harvin sidelined, Jermaine Kearse, a former University of Washington receiver from Tacoma, not only caught a 12-yard touchdown pass from Wilson, but returned a kickoff 107 yards for a touchdown, one of two 100-yard plays made by the Seahawks. Brandon Browner returned a fumble 106 yards, one of four turnovers the Seahawks forced upon the Broncos. To Carroll's delight, his team left CenturyLink Field without a turnover.

"The most important factor that's happening right now is that we're not giving the football up," Carroll said after Seattle's 40–10 blowout victory over the favorites to win the AFC. "That's how we intend to play forever."

Despite allowing 182 penalty yards, the Seahawks slogged out an ugly 17–10 victory over Green Bay at Lambeau Field in the third preseason game. In the final exhibition, they had no trouble handling Oakland, thanks to three scoring drives by Tarvaris Jackson, and that enabled him to beat out Quinn for the backup job to Wilson.

"The best thing about the preseason is that we did a fantastic job of taking care of the ball," Carroll said. "We were plus-eight in turnovers. That's our formula: play tough on offense, defense, and special teams and take care of the ball. If we do that, we'll win a lot of games. Now, we're ready to go." ■

In many ways, Russell Wilson was the perfect Pete Carroll player. He had a keen interest in the nature of success, one of Carroll's favorite topics. (Photo by Drew Sellers)

CHAPTER 6

THE SEASON: GOALS MET

Cheered on by a Sea Gal, Russell Wilson takes the field for the Seahawks' first home game of the 2013 season against the 49ers. (Photo by Drew McKenzie)

SEAHAWKS START SEASON 4-0

Seattle Pummels Rival 49ers in Week 2

Wizards of odds established the Seahawks 3½-point picks over Cam Newton and the Carolina Panthers. Not much of a spread there, but a significant one considering the Seahawks would be playing in Charlotte's Bank of America Stadium against the eventual NFC South champions. So confident were swamis that Seattle received the Week 1 betting nod despite an 8–17 record over the previous six seasons in games in the Eastern time zone that kicked off at 10 AM, Pacific Time.

"I'm glad they've got a buzz. I'm glad they're feeling good," Carolina defensive end Greg Hardy said. "But if they don't block, don't run, and don't score, they don't win."

SEPTEMBER 8 AT CHARLOTTE: SEAHAWKS 12, PANTHERS 7

Russell Wilson absorbed his worst beating as a pro with two sacks, six hits, and 11 hurries but produced his first 300-yard regular-season game, finishing 25-of-33 for 320 yards, one touchdown, no interceptions, and a 115.7 rating.

Wilson eluded multiple sack attempts, notably in the third quarter when he made the equivalent of a full-court basketball shot by avoiding sacks at least twice and, almost 20 yards behind the line of scrimmage, flung the ball off his back foot a moment before he was splattered. About 50 yards later along the sideline, wide receiver Doug Baldwin grabbed the ball and came down barely in bounds. The improbable play set up a field goal that closed Carolina's lead to 7–6.

"After the first five or six passes, he was on fire," Pete Carroll said. "He made a ton of plays. Finding Doug on the sidelines, that was ridiculous…With Russell now, we don't have to hold anything back."

SEPTEMBER 15 AT SEATTLE: SEAHAWKS 29, 49ERS 3

At 136 decibels the party at CenturyLink set a Guinness world record for din. At 121 yards in penalties, the San Francisco 49ers made a run at setting a mark for dumb. At 29–3 the Seahawks made a run at explaining what their deal was.

The deal: dance.

Whether it was Marshawn Lynch's mocking sashays across the goal line (he scored on runs of 14 and 2 yards and added a 7-yard touchdown catch), Richard Sherman's post-interception choreography along the sideline with the SeaGals, the locker-room groove-fest during a long weather delay, or whether it was the collective stomp upon the 49ers' heads, the Seahawks' deal was all about high-steppin'.

Russell Wilson carried 10 times for 33 yards and passed for 142 yards in the Seahawks' 29–3 win over the rival 49ers on September 15, 2013. (Photo by Drew McKenzie)

In front of a Sunday night national TV audience supported by the loudest fans (68,338) ever jammed into the joint, the Seahawks laid a triumphant Ta-da upon their archrivals.

"What a frickin' night!" coach Pete Carroll said. "What an amazing night for the 12th Man. Unbelievable."

Russell Wilson threw incomplete on eight of his first nine passes, took a shower during a freakish 60-minute weather delay, and came back out looking, according to Sherman, like a "baaaad maaan!"

After the teams played the first 5-0 halftime in the NFL in 21 years, Wilson led the Seahawks on two touchdown drives. The rout was conclusively on. Sherman made his case for All-Pro, holding Anquan Boldin to one catch for seven yards.

SEPTEMBER 22 AT SEATTLE:
SEAHAWKS 45, JAGUARS 17

Yes, the opponent was Jacksonville, barely a lounge act on the NFL stage. But the Jaguars set up well the main act. Wilson matched his career high with four touchdown passes, including a pair each to tight end Zach Miller and wide receiver Sidney Rice. The Seahawks won their 10th in a row at home and notched a 3-0 start for the first time since 2006.

Wilson dazzled in the final minute of the first half. With Jacksonville on the Seattle 18, the Seahawks were on the verge of giving up a touchdown for the first time in seven quarters. Instead the defense pressured quarterback Chad Henne into throwing a ball off his center's helmet. Linebacker Bobby Wagner intercepted the carom, leaving 44 seconds and 79 yards for Wilson, who only needed 34 to take the Seahawks to a touchdown and a 24-0 lead.

SEPTEMBER 29 AT HOUSTON:
SEAHAWKS 23, TEXANS 20 (OT)

The only way the Seahawks could have been deader at halftime was finding 53 toe tags in the locker room. Overwhelmed by the hyper-aggressive Texans, the Seahawks were down 20-6 with eight minutes left. But behind Wilson, the dead men walked, ran, and then exulted, stunning Houston with a rally to tie in regulation and an overtime field goal to win.

The Seahawks had never been 4-0, and no 4-0 team reached that benchmark in a more flabbergasting manner.

All-Pro J.J. Watt and mates hit or sacked Wilson on 16-of-34 dropbacks. But Wilson came through with one memorable stretch, orchestrating a seven-minute, 14-play, 98-yard drive that actually covered 113 yards, counting ground lost via penalties. The score was a three-yard pass from Wilson to Marshawn Lynch, cutting the Houston lead to 20-13 with 7:43 left. Richard Sherman knotted it at 20 when he picked off suddenly erratic quarterback Matt Schaub and ran 58 yards, sans a shoe, forcing overtime. The Seahawks went home elated after Steven Hauschka's game-winning field goal.

On only four other occasions in franchise history had the Seahawks overcome a larger deficit to win (the greatest was 20 points behind at Denver in 1995), but Wilson could have had a bigger brag if he'd known about it. In 37 seasons and three games before meeting Houston, the Seahawks had overcome a 13-point fourth-quarter deficit to win three times but had never overcome a deficit as large as 14 in 105 chances, proving that where there was Wilson, there was a way. ■

SEATTLE'S GREATEST FOURTH QUARTER COMEBACKS

Year	Date	Opponent	Deficit	Fourth Quarter
2013	September 29	Texans	14	Trailed 20-6, won with FG in OT
1999	September 19	Bears	13	Trailed 13-0, won on Glen Foley's TD pass
2002	December 29	Chargers	13	Trailed 20-7, won on Ryan Lindell's FG in OT
2003	October 19	Bears	13	Trailed 17-6, won on Shaun Alexander's TD

Safety Earl Thomas came to the Seahawks as the 14th overall pick in the 2010 NFL draft. He became a three-time Pro Bowler. (Photo by Drew Sellers)

RUN, RUSSELL, RUN!

Wilson Shines Despite O-line Injuries

With starting tackles Russell Okung and Breno Giacomini out with injuries and center Max Unger also sidelined, Russell Wilson found himself under assault every week in games 5 through 8. The Cardinals dinged Wilson 19 times in Week 7 and the Rams leveled him seven times in Week 8. At the season's midpoint, Wilson had been sacked 27 times, six shy of the 33 take-downs he suffered as a rookie. Hit or hurried more than 12 times per game, Wilson was fortunate to be blessed with the quickness and speed to avoid a season-ending injury.

OCTOBER 6 AT INDIANAPOLIS: COLTS 34, SEAHAWKS 28

Settling four times for field goals instead of touch-downs, the Seahawks' offense, missing four starters, didn't have the firepower to win another road game, ending a club-record 4–0 start. The absences of offensive linemen Unger, Okung, and Giacomini and tight end Zach Miller cost the Seahawks inside the 30-yard line and forced Wilson to scramble far more than Carroll wanted.

A 12–0 first-quarter Seattle lead slowly crumbled under Indianapolis quarterback Andrew Luck's increas-ing prowess. Seventeen second-half Colts points included a rare block of a Seahawks field goal attempt returned 61 yards for a touchdown, a potential 10-point swing.

Wilson passed for 210 yards and ran for a career-high 102 with seven runs of 10 yards or longer. The Wilson vs. Luck matchup went as advertised, so close in individual performance that at the 6:38 mark of the fourth quarter both had identical passing lines: 15-of-27 for 210 yards, two touchdowns, and no interceptions.

Wilson became the fifth player in NFL history to pass for 200 and rush for 100 in a losing effort, joining Oakland's Terrelle Pryor (2013), Philadelphia's Donovan McNabb (2002), San Francisco's Steve Young (1990), and Green Bay's Tobin Rote (1951 and 1952).

OCTOBER 13 VS. TENNESSEE: SEAHAWKS 20, TITANS 13

So many people did so many wrong things for Seattle, including a botched field-goal attempt that resulted in a 77-yard touchdown return for the Titans, that it seemed like Murphy's Law.

But the Seahawks received 155 yards and two touch-downs from Marshawn Lynch, and Richard Sherman's third interception of the season made the difference.

The Seahawks needed all 60 minutes to put away the no-excitement Titans and did so only with a 10-point surge in the fourth quarter.

Russell Wilson prepares to leave CenturyLink Field after leading the Seahawks to a 20–13 win over the Tennessee Titans on October 13, 2013. (Photo by Drew McKenzie)

Wilson did not throw a touchdown or an interception but completed 23-of-31 passes for 257 yards and a 98.5 rating. That included Wilson averaging 11.1 yards per attempt after play-action fakes vs. 4.9 yards on all other passes. As he had in other recent games, Wilson did more with his legs, rushing for 61 yards on 10 carries. Four of his rushes resulted in first downs.

OCTOBER 17 AT ARIZONA: SEAHAWKS 34, CARDINALS 22

The Cardinals strip-sacked Wilson into two lost fumbles that turned into 14 Arizona points. But when his depleted offensive line allowed him to operate, Wilson delivered another boffo performance, completing 18-of-29 passes for 235 yards, three touchdowns, no interceptions, and a passer rating of 122.1.

"He's a highlight film waiting to happen," said head coach Pete Carroll. "He has the broadest spectrum [of playmaking] of all the [quarterbacks] I've had. He's a pretty fun guy to have."

On passes that traveled at least 15 yards downfield, Wilson completed 71 percent, including two touchdowns. His 31-yard touchdown to Sidney Rice marked his sixth career touchdown that traveled at least 30 yards.

One play underscored Carroll's point about Wilson being a fun guy to have. In the third quarter, Wilson scrambled on third down and was run down by a tackler who had Wilson's legs wrapped up. As Wilson fell, he kept his head and arm up and a moment before he slammed down flicked a short shovel pass that diving tight end Zach Miller caught for a first down.

By the end of the game, Wilson had 20 or more rushing attempts in a four-game span eight times (top six listed below). No other Seattle quarterback was remotely close.

OCTOBER 28 AT ST. LOUIS: SEAHAWKS 14, RAMS 9

The *Monday Night Football* game in the sparsely populated Edward Jones Dome—the World Series was going on across the street—was a big pile of nothing. But the Seahawks prevailed because they made one good offensive play—an 80-yard touchdown from Wilson to Golden Tate—and one good goal-line stand. Most of the rest could have been set curbside for pickup by the big green trucks.

The Rams ran seven plays in the red zone in the final 1:23, including five inside the Seattle six-yard line, but couldn't get the ball in the end zone. The final play was a pass from quarterback Kellen Clemens intended for wide receiver Brian Quick that sailed over his—and cornerback Brandon Browner's—head as time expired.

The Rams sacked Wilson seven times, a career high, three each by ends Robert Quinn and Chris Long. Undeterred, Wilson also threw a two-yard touchdown to Tate.

Snapshot of Wilson's night: in one sequence, Wilson dropped to pass five times and was sacked four.

Only one quarterback in franchise history went down more times than 27 in a season's first eight contests—Dave Krieg, who suffered 29 sacks in the first eight of 1985. ■

MOST RUSHING ATTEMPTS (ANY FOUR-GAME SPAN) BY A SEAHAWKS QUARTERBACK

Year	Span	Quarterback	Att.	Skinny
2013	September 29–October 17	Russell Wilson	41	1st 100-yard rush game at Indy
2012	November 4–December 2	Russell Wilson	30	7.6 yards per attempt at Miami
2012	December 9–30	Russell Wilson	28	6.7 yard-average in four games
2012	December 2–23	Russell Wilson	27	Rushed for three TDs at Buffalo
2013	September 8–29	Russell Wilson	27	10 attempts vs. 49ers, Texans
2012	November 4–December 2	Russell Wilson	26	127.3 pass rating vs. Vikings
1993	September 26–October 24	Rick Mirer	22	Season-high nine rushes at Cincy

A nearly prone Russell Wilson gets off a pass while being tackled during the Seahawks' 34–22 victory over Arizona at University of Phoenix Stadium Oct. 17, 2013. (Photo by Drew McKenzie)

"NEXT MAN UP"

Seahawks Sweep Through November With Impressive Victories

Although the Seahawks lost cornerback Walter Thurmond to a four-game suspension and faced the prospect of losing to suspension cornerback Brandon Browner for the second time in two years, Wilson kept the Seahawks undefeated in the four games of the season's third quarter. Following Seattle's victory against Minnesota in Week 11, coupled with Denver's second-half collapse in a 34–31 overtime loss at New England, Las Vegas oddsmakers tabbed the Seahawks, originally 10–1, as 3–1 favorites to win Super Bowl XLVIII. Following a blowout win against the Saints in Week 13, national media began hyping Wilson as a possible MVP candidate.

NOVEMBER 3 AT SEATTLE:
SEAHAWKS 27, BUCCANEERS 24

Given a 21-point deficit, 200 rushing yards allowed, and a -3 turnover margin, the Seahawks should have crawled out of CenturyLink Field smarting from their first home loss in two years—and to a 16½-point underdog. But for the first time in the franchise's 37 years and 610 regular-season and playoff games, the Seahawks overcame a deficit of more than 20 points and strutted off a winner on Steven Hauschka's 27-yard field goal 4:48 into overtime.

Wilson had a 25.0 passer rating after one quarter and a 58.3 mark at halftime, but ended up completing 19 of 26 for 217 yards, two touchdowns, and two interceptions for a final rating of 91.3 to complement Marshawn Lynch, who ran for 125 yards, his 18th 100-yard game in 33 outings.

Wilson suffered no sacks but was hit six times, continuing his status as the most-rocked quarterback in the NFL. To put a finer point on it, Wilson found himself under duress on a career-high 55 percent of his dropbacks (16-of-29) but somehow threw both of his touchdowns and gained 125 of his passing yards when hit or hurried.

NOVEMBER 10 AT ATLANTA:
SEAHAWKS 33, FALCONS 10

Despite continuing offensive line injuries, the Seahawks put together their most comprehensive beat down of the season, scoring seven times in their first eight possessions. Wilson improved to 20–6 as a starting quarterback, two wins shy of Ben Roethlisberger's NFL record for most in the first two seasons of a career, after completing 19-of-26 passes for 287 yards and two touchdowns with no interceptions for a rating of 134.6. The Falcons sacked Wilson just once.

Trickeration play of the season: Marshawn Lynch took a handoff from Wilson for a sweep right, stopped, and threw back to Wilson, who unloaded a 43-yard bomb in the end zone to wide receiver Jermaine Kearse, who beat good coverage to the catch.

Only one other NFL team in the previous 20 seasons recorded a road victory by as large a margin as Seattle's

Protected by offensive linemen Paul McQuistan (67) and J.R. Sweezy (64), Russell Wilson completed 19 of 26 passes for 217 yards and two touchdowns in Seattle's 27–24 victory over Tampa Bay Nov. 3, 2013. (Photo by Drew McKenzie)

23-point edge against a team that ousted it from the previous year's playoffs. That team was another edition of Carroll's—the 2010 Seahawks, who lost to the Bears 35–24 in the divisional playoffs, then came back to Soldier Field and knocked off Chicago 38–14, a 24-point swing.

NOVEMBER 17 AT SEATTLE:
SEAHAWKS 41, VIKINGS 20

The Seahawks finally declared all of their injured players ready, including Percy Harvin, out since training camp. Harvin did not get lot of plays (16) but dazzled with two. He made a bobbling, tumbling grab of a Wilson pass for a 17-yard catch that set up Seattle's second touchdown and returned his first kickoff as a Seahawk 58 yards that set up the third score.

The Seahawks needed Wilson for only three quarters, during which he completed 13-of-18 passes for 230 yards, two touchdowns, and no interceptions for a season-best rating of 151.4.

Wilson's rating was also the second highest delivered by a Seattle quarterback, a couple of points shy of Dave Krieg's 153.3 against San Diego on December 14, 1986.

Wilson, who threw a 19-yard touchdown to Doug Baldwin and flipped a six-yard touchdown to Marshawn Lynch, recorded his 21st win as a starting quarterback, one shy of Ben Roethlisberger's mark for most wins in the first two seasons of a career. Wilson had four completions of 20 yards or more and connected with nine receivers before taking a seat.

That brought to 28 for the season Wilson's number of 20-yard+ completions, a mark trailing only Drew Brees (36), Andrew Luck (35), Joe Flacco (35), Peyton Manning (33), and Matthew Stafford (29).

DECEMBER 2 AT SEATTLE:
SEAHAWKS 34, SAINTS 7

A matchup of New Orleans' second-ranked passing offense vs. Seattle's No. 2-rated pass defense had the NFL abuzz for *Monday Night Football*. But the drama never materialized. The Saints did not get a first down until the last minute of the first quarter, when they were behind 17–0. They finished with 44 yards rushing. Quarterback Drew Brees threw eight passes that went 15 yards beyond the line of scrimmage, and completed none. No one said "Aints" out loud, but every fan at CenturyLink Field on a stormy night surely thought it.

The Seahawks, becoming the first team to produce eight wins by 20 or more points during a home winning streak of at least 14 games since the 1972–73 Miami Dolphins, held All-Pro Brees to a meager 147 passing yards, snapping a Brees streak of 43 consecutive games, an NFL record, with at least 200.

Meanwhile, Wilson had almost no flaws. He completed 22-of-30 passes for 310 yards, three touchdowns, and no interceptions for a rating of 139.6. On passes aimed 10 or more yards down the field, Wilson went 7-for-10 for 203 yards, including a touchdown to Doug Baldwin.

Wilson also led Seattle in rushing with 47 yards on eight carries. Wilson surpassed 300 passing yards for the third time in his career in running his record as a starting quarterback to 22–6, matching Ben Roethlisberger's NFL record for most wins in the first two seasons. ■

Russell Wilson, also shown on the big screen at CenturyLink Field, scores on a 10-yard run against the Tampa Bay Bucs November 3, 2013. (Photo by Drew McKenzie)

BUMPY ROUTE TO THE FINISH

Seahawks Lose 2, Wilson Has Most Wins for 2nd-Year QB

Instead of closing the regular season with an inspiring flourish, the Seahawks—and Wilson—struggled over the final quarter, twice failing to wrap up the NFC West when presented the chance. The Seahawks went 2–2, and Wilson threw almost as many interceptions (three) as touchdowns (four). In only one game, December 29 vs. St. Louis, did Wilson exceed a 100.0 passer rating, and in that game managed a meager 172 yards.

Seattle's struggles stemmed from a difficult schedule and matchup problems opponents presented. Three of the four were division games as the NFC West emerged the NFL's toughest division.

DECEMBER 8 AT SAN FRANCISCO: 49ERS 19, SEAHAWKS 17

The Seahawks entered their rivalry showdown at Candlestick Park having blistered the 49ers by a combined 71–16 in two previous meetings—both at CenturyLink. But the Seahawks lost four in a row at The Stick by a combined 109–54, though the most recent defeat there, October 18, 2012, was close, 13–6.

So was the second matchup of 2013. It, too, did not go Seattle's way. The Seahawks self-destructed with nine penalties and a blocked punt. The mistakes butchered a winnable game not decided until Frank Gore's 51-yard run

off guard late in the fourth quarter set up Phil Dawson's game-winning 22-yard field goal.

In quarterbacking only his second loss of the season, Wilson completed 15-of-25 passes for 199 yards and a touchdown, but a late interception on an attempted 70-yard Hail Mary to Jermaine Kearse dropped his passer rating for the day to 81.9, breaking a streak of three consecutive 100.0+ efforts.

Ever in pursuit of a silver lining, Carroll embraced the notion that the Seahawks' loss was useful in terms of dope-slapping any smugness his team may have developed in the 11–1 start.

"It can help if you utilize it," Carroll said. "It's a learning opportunity. I like (other teams) to learn the hard way, but that's not always the case."

DECEMBER 15 AT NEW YORK: SEAHAWKS 23, GIANTS 0

Billed as a Super Bowl dress rehearsal for the team with the NFL's best record, the Seahawks did little to disappoint those anticipating a return to MetLife Stadium by delivering the first hometown shutout of the Giants in 18 years.

Neither the Seahawks nor Wilson did much offensively, but the defense tortured Eli Manning into five interceptions while sacking him three times. Wilson threw for 206 yards—73 on six throws to Marshawn Lynch—one

Russell Wilson greets New York quarterback Eli Manning at MetLife Stadium after Wilson led the Seahawks to a 23–0 victory on December 15, 2013. The Seahawks intercepted Manning five times in the rout. (Photo by Drew McKenzie)

touchdown and one interception and improved his record to 6–1 following a loss.

Wilson set an NFL record with his 23rd victory, breaking Ben Roethlisberger's previous mark of 22 for most by a starting quarterback in his first two seasons. Wilson's 50th career touchdown pass, a 12-yarder to Doug Baldwin, also enabled him to join Dan Marino (68) and Peyton Manning (52) as the only quarterbacks to toss 50 or more in their first two years.

"These are marks this guy [Wilson] is going to continue to knock off," Carroll said. "It's really cool that he's been able to do that, and he still has a couple of games left."

Wilson didn't seem concerned about individual records.

"The biggest thing is that we'll have a great feel for the stadium," Wilson said with his eye focused on the Super Bowl. "We were successful here. You get good vibes if we get to come back. It's a great place to play."

DECEMBER 22 AT SEATTLE:
CARDINALS 17, SEAHAWKS 10

Wilson never had a bad day until he ran into vastly improved Arizona in Week 15. In the aftermath the temptation was to blame his offensive line, receivers, Marshawn Lynch, Pete Carroll, offensive coordinator Darrell Bevell, the Legion of Boom, and even the Mariners, Seattle's default civic punching bag.

But Wilson would have none of it. He completed 11-of-27 passes for 108 yards, one touchdown, and one pick, which shackled him with a 49.6 rating, his worst as a pro. Sacking him four times and containing him in the pocket, the Cardinals prevented Wilson's havoc-creating edge plays.

"Sometimes you just have a bad day," said Wilson, losing for the first time in 14 career games at the Clink. "Hopefully, you can get rid of those days."

For once, Wilson found himself on the wrong end of history. When Arizona's Carson Palmer—one touchdown pass, four interceptions—threw a 31-yard touchdown to Michael Floyd over Byron Maxwell with 2:13 remaining for the winning points, he became the first quarterback in 60 years to toss a game-winning touchdown in the last three minutes of the fourth quarter after hurling four or more interceptions without a touchdown prior to that.

DECEMBER 29 AT SEATTLE:
SEAHAWKS 27, RAMS 9

In a flag fest at the Clink, the Seahawks and Rams combined for 19 penalties, including five unsportsmanlike calls on the Rams. Four were tossed on one play in the first half—three on St. Louis, one on Seattle—and three more were whistled against St. Louis on one play in the second half.

At one point in the third quarter, the Cardinals had more yards lost to penalties than yards gained on offense.

In a maelstrom of boiling tempers and lost heads, Wilson kept his, enabling the Seahawks to finish 13–3, matching a franchise best by the 2005 team.

The Seahawks also won for the 20th time in 24 games with Wilson at quarterback. He had an efficient outing, connecting on 15-of-23 passes for 172 yards and a 102.0 passer rating, including a 47-yard touchdown to Golden Tate that delivered the knockout blow at 9:23 of the fourth quarter as Seattle took a 27–3 lead.

Inelegant as the season sometimes was, the Seahawks waded through injuries, controversies over drug busts, the Percy Harvin injury soap opera, and a late-season offensive slowdown to become the No. 1 seed in the NFC. But even that came with baggage. ■

Seattle capped its 27–9 victory over the St. Louis Rams with a 47-yard touchdown pass from Russell Wilson to wide receiver Golden Tate early in the fourth quarter. Tate caught eight passes for 129 yards. (Photo by Drew Sellers)

CHAPTER 7

HOME FOR THE PLAYOFFS

Russell Wilson hands to Marshawn Lynch (24), who gained 109 yards and scored a touchdown in Seattle's 23–17 NFC Championship victory over San Francisco on January 19, 2014. (Photo by Drew McKenzie)

SAINTS PLAY ROUGH, SEAHAWKS PLAY BETTER

On Blustery Night, Wilson Makes No Mistakes

After four years and more than 1,000 player transactions under general manager John Schneider and head coach Pete Carroll, the Seahawks found themselves in prime position. Closing out a 13–3 regular season with a 27–9 victory over the St. Louis Rams, Seattle was division champion, the No. 1 seed, and had home-field advantage throughout the playoffs. Two more home wins and the Seahawks would be off to MetLife Stadium for Super Bowl XLVIII.

The road seemed straightforward, but held numerous traps. Since 2002, 12 teams, including the 15–1 2011 Green Bay Packers, finished a regular season with a record of 13–3 or better. All were favored, by at least four points, to win their divisional playoff game. All had lost on their home fields, abruptly ending their Super Bowl aspirations.

Since 1978, when the NFL adopted the 16-game schedule, the league had crowned 234 division champions. Eighty-one (34.6 percent) went one-and-done in the postseason. Since 2002, 35 of 96 division champions—36.4 percent—lost in either the wild card or divisional round.

A great regular-season record didn't seem to matter much. Nor did favorable seeding. Twenty-one No. 1 seeds since 1990 had reached the Super Bowl, but only two No. 1s in the past decade had won it.

With all that, the Seahawks didn't have the luxury of buying into the confidence of oddsmakers, who established them as eight-point picks to beat the New Orleans Saints. A lot had changed since Seattle's 34–7 romp on December 2.

Although the Saints barely made the playoffs, grabbing the No. 6 seed, they shed the tag as a soft dome team. In a tough venue in Philadelphia, the Saints the previous week won the franchise's first playoff game on the road. And no one had to be reminded how Arizona three weeks earlier shattered Seattle's presumption of invincibility at home.

For the Seahawks, the main thing, as far as Pete Carroll was concerned, was to adopt the attitude that the previous game with the Saints never happened.

"What has happened in the past doesn't tell the story of what's going to happen in the future, one way or the other,'" said Carroll. "We have to be focused on what's up right now."

The rematch did not resemble Seattle's Week 13 blowout, except for the fact that it was again contested in blustery conditions.

Wilson contributed to Seattle's 23–15 victory mainly by not making big mistakes. Hampered by wind gusts up to 45 mph that played havoc with passes, he completed only 9-of-18 for 103 yards and no touchdowns—but no picks. Three of Wilson's nine misses came on short crossing routes not hampered by wind, the pass rush, or defensive backs. Wilson managed conditions as best he could, allowing Marshawn Lynch to do to the Saints what he did to them in the 2010 playoffs: Go seismic.

Marshawn Lynch tumbles into the end zone in the Seahawks' playoff win over the New Orleans Saints. Lynch rushed for 140 yards on 28 carries and scored two touchdowns. (Photo by Drew Sellers)

That moment came with 2:40 left and Seattle holding a 16–8 lead. Seattle's O-line caved the Saints' front, Lynch took the handoff, bounced outside and, behind a key block from Jermaine Kearse, went 31 yards for the winning score, a not-quite-as-lengthy re-run of the 67-yard "Beast Quake" play that became a YouTube megastar. The play provoked a hallelujah chorus from 68,388 Clinksters, who began turning their attention to the San Francisco-Carolina game.

While Lynch set a franchise playoff record with 140 rushing yards, Wilson's bottom line would have looked markedly better with two additional completions. On the Seahawks' third offensive play, Percy Harvin, in action for the first time since the Minnesota game November 17, had a 30-yard gain in his grasp, but took an illegal blow to the head from Saints safety Rafael Bush, who received a 15-yard penalty for targeting a defenseless receiver. Harvin had to be guided to the sideline for an exam, but returned in 10 minutes.

Then, with a shade under two minutes left in the first half, Seattle moved inside the Saints' 10 before stalling. On second down, Wilson threw a near-perfect lob to the corner of the end zone for which Harvin leaped and touched but couldn't haul in. His prone body hit head first, hard. He left for the sidelines and another concussion check. This time, he was done for the day.

The Saints entered the game thinking they could win if they accomplished three things: Limit Lynch on the ground, manage the crowd noise, and avoid turnovers. New Orleans handled the din better than in Week 13—Drew Brees completed 24-of-43 passes for 309 yards, one touchdown, and no interceptions—but 1-for-3 didn't cut it. Lynch gained 66 of his yards after contact.

What the Saints didn't count on was Brees' inability to find tight end Jimmy Graham, who caught one pass for eight yards after catching three balls in the first meeting.

Since winning it all in 2009, three of the Saints' four seasons died in the Pacific hinterlands—twice in Seattle, once in San Francisco. Their latest West Coast buzzkill didn't even require much from Wilson. But his flagging accuracy brought worries that grew largest for the biggest game yet—a third seasonal meeting with the San Francisco 49ers. ■

Above: Russell Wilson completed 9 of 18 passes for 109 yards in Seattle's 23-15 victory over New Orleans in an NFC divisional playoff game on January 11, 2014. Opposite: Golden Tate leaps to make a 13-yard catch against the New Orleans Saints in Seattle's 23-15 NFC divisional playoff victory. (Photos by Drew McKenzie)

WILSON WINS DEBATE

Wilson Convinces Carroll; Seahawks Out-Smart 49ers

At the apex moment of a sports season, the task of the fan is to over-think, over-worry, and over-react. The engagement is hormonal, so the fan's primary instinct is abject fear. It is the task of the participant athlete to do the opposite—trust instinct and practice and allow the training to come out without thinking.

As the Seahawks prepared to meet the San Francisco 49ers in the NFC Championship, quarterback Russell Wilson was asked to address the chief angst of fans, who had observed his diminishing production in the passing game and worked themselves into a state of doomsday anxiety.

Naturally, they demanded answers. But if they also sought some sort of deep revelation, Wilson's remarks fell woefully short.

"I think," said Wilson, "the biggest thing is to be more accurate on a couple of throws I normally make. It's nothing I need to search deep down for, or go study a whole bunch for. It's just: Put the ball on the money, right where it needs to be."

Wilson's career since high school had been on an unbroken upward trajectory, making him partly a victim of his own success. It was also true that he had experienced a temporary performance decline due to defenses catching up to his style of success, including limiting his chances to run from the pocket.

Question was, could Wilson make adjustments in time for the 49ers? San Francisco had won eight in a row since a 23–20 loss to New Orleans in the Superdome on November 17, including 23–20 and 23–10 road playoff wins at Green Bay and Carolina, while the Seahawks had seemingly flattened out.

And even if Wilson made those adjustments, could he get a grip on his nerves with the Super Bowl at stake? He had always been unflappable, but this was a bigger stage than any he'd encountered—a frenzied home crowd adrenalized by the most significant, thrilling matchup in Seattle pro sports history, which also captivated the nation.

Apart from the sharp contrast between Jim Harbaugh and Pete Carroll, two coaches as different as a one-room schoolhouse and an Internet café, not much separated the Seahawks and 49ers. In 16 regular-season games, Seattle scored 45 touchdowns, San Francisco 44. The Seahawks averaged 26.1 points, the 49ers 25.4. The Seahawks allowed an average of 14.4 points, the Niners 17.0. The Seahawks had more interceptions (28 to 18) and a better turnover differential (+20 to San Francisco's +12), but the Niners had been better against the run (95.9 yards allowed per game to 101.6) and yielded fewer sacks (39 to Seattle's 44).

Due to the home-field edge, the Seahawks were made 3½-point favorites, but that turned out to be wildly

Russell Wilson hoists the NFC Championship trophy after the Seahawks defeated the San Francisco 49ers 23–17 at CenturyLink Field on January 19, 2014. Wilson threw the game-winning touchdown pass of 35 yards to Jermaine Kearse. (Photo by Drew Sellers)

generous against a team in its third consecutive NFC title match. In a game that began with Wilson suffering a strip sack deep in his own territory that made the entirety of CenturyLink shudder, the outcome came down to one moment, certain to be replayed for Seattle audiences as often as Mariner Edgar Martinez's 1995 double beat the Yankees in the playoffs.

Thirty seconds were left and the 49ers trailed 23–17, but they had a first-and-10 at the Seattle 18. Fans were standing, screaming, imploring a final play from the Seattle defense that delivered so many times. Quarterback Colin Kaepernick dropped back quickly and lobbed a fade to standout receiver Michael Crabtree in the right corner of the end zone. Crabtree leaped. A catch would all but seal a trip to the Super Bowl.

But cornerback Richard Sherman soared in front of him. He stretched and reached the ball first, pushing it back toward the field to a teammate, Malcolm Smith, who gathered in the interception. A week of high anxiety in Seattle evaporated, replaced by euphoria.

But the dramatic moment in one of the most compelling playoff games in recent NFL history wouldn't have happened if Carroll a little earlier hadn't acquiesced to his second-year quarterback.

Trailing 17–13 early in the fourth quarter, facing a fourth-and-7 at the San Francisco 35, the Seahawks had three choices: a punt, a 53-yard field goal, or going for it against a defense that had bludgeoned them most of the game.

"We were trying to figure out what to do," Wilson said. "I was kind of begging (Carroll) on the sidelines, hey, let's go for it. And he decided we were going for it."

Armed with the breathtaking decision, Wilson went to the huddle and called the pass. Then he issued an alert.

"Hey, listen, we're going to go double-count right here," he said, referring to a change in cadence of the snap count. "Hopefully, they go off-sides. If they do, we take a shot down the field because it's a free play."

Sure enough, they did.

San Francisco defensive end Aldon Smith jumped from his left end slot just enough that he was caught across the line when the ball was snapped. Flags went up, but the play was allowed to go on, as Wilson hoped. Dropping back under pressure, he sent a laser straight down the middle to receiver Jermaine Kearse in the end zone.

The kid they call "Chop Chop," from Tacoma's Lakes High and the University of Washington, became a featured part of Northwest sports history when he found a small space in a tightly defended window for a catch that put Seattle ahead, 20–17, for the first time in the game.

On fourth-and-7, they had perfect execution. The play was a dagger into the 49ers, who jumped on the Seahawks and their annoying partisans with a 10–0 lead, largely because of Kaepernick's legs (130 yards rushing, long of 58). But the Seahawks inexorably crept back until Wilson insisted his team wait for the deke and then go long.

"We had a great call and an incredible play by Russell and the protection," Carroll said. "And Kearse came through with a heroic touchdown."

After Sherman's tip to Smith, after Wilson (16 of 25, 215 yards, 104.6 rating) took the final snap in triumph, and following Sherman's nationally televised rant on FOX directed at Crabtree, Wilson acknowledged two thoughts.

"To be honest, at the last snap," he said, smiling, "I was thinking I could have been playing baseball right now. The other thing I thought about was just all the people who told me I couldn't do it, who told me I couldn't get there."

None were among the 68,454 celebrants rocking the house when Wilson took a final knee. They had just done the math: 12th man, plus 53 on the roster, multiplied by 5'11" = XLVIII. ■

Russell Wilson threw for 215 yards and a touchdown in Seattle's 23–17 NFC Championship victory over San Francisco. (Photo by Drew McKenzie)

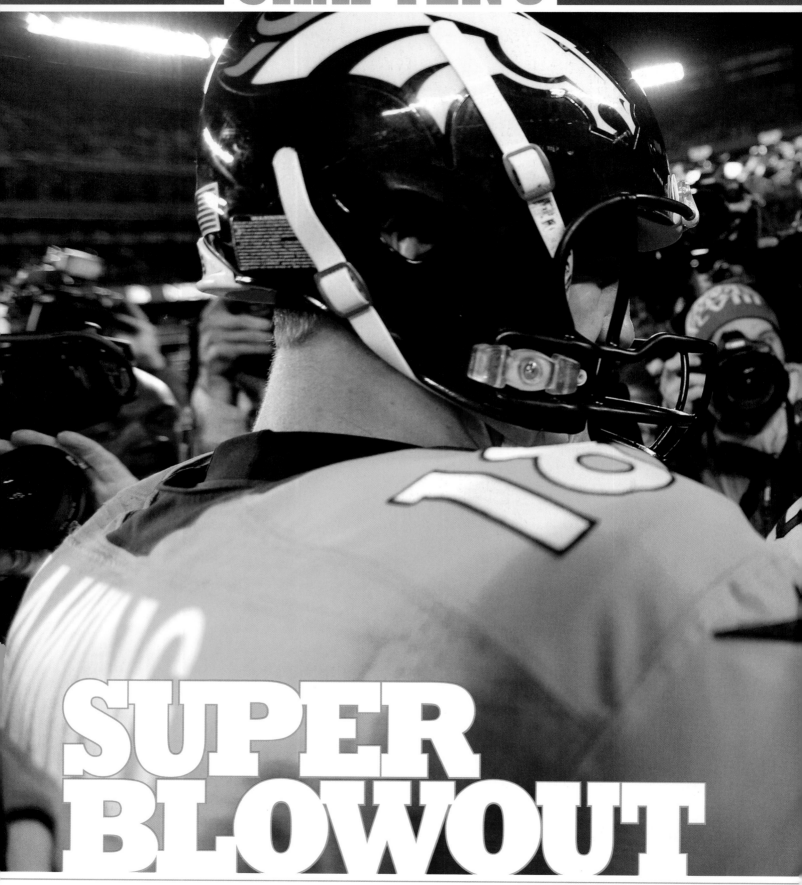

CHAPTER 8

SUPER BLOWOUT

Quarterbacks Peyton Manning and Russell Wilson shake hands after the Seahawks' dominant 43–8 win over Manning's Denver Broncos in Super Bowl XLVIII. (AP Images)

DRAMA ON THE BIGGEST STAGE

Wilson Could Have Been Manning's Backup Instead of Foe

Russell Wilson had an opportunity in the spring of 2012 to become the heir to Peyton Manning in Denver, but came up short—by nearly a foot. Prior to that year's draft, when Wilson ultimately went 75th overall in the third round to the Seahawks, the Broncos wanted to select a quarterback that could succeed Manning after he retired. As the draft reached the second round, they narrowed their options to Wilson and Arizona State's Brock Osweiler.

Broncos executive vice president of football operations John Elway later conceded to ESPN an infatuation with Wilson, impressed by his athleticism, attitude and, most of all, his ability to extend plays.

"We had him in (Broncos headquarters) and we loved the kid," Elway told ESPN. "You knew when you met him that he had the capability because of the presence that he has."

But…Elway also believed that in order to be successful in the NFL, a quarterback needed to be taller than Wilson's 5'10 $^5/_8$". That pushed Elway toward Osweiler, a 6'8", 240-pound pocket passer who once verbally committed to play basketball for Gonzaga.

For Elway, the foot difference in height between Wilson and Osweiler was one of two key separators. The other: Osweiler was 21, Wilson 23.

By January 19, 2014, when Manning led Denver to a 26–16 victory over Tom Brady and the New England Patriots in the AFC Championship, Osweiler appeared in nine NFL games in two years while Wilson became a two-time Pro Bowler and quarterback of the NFC's No. 1-seeded team. Elway would soon get another chance to revisit his decision.

The Seattle-Denver matchup would mark the first Super Bowl since the New York Giants defeated Buffalo 20–19 following the 1990 season that the NFL's top-ranked offense (Denver) would face the top-ranked defense (Seattle). It would be only the second time in 20 years that a pair of No. 1 seeds would battle for the Lombardi Trophy.

Oddsmakers installed the AFC Broncos as three-point favorites largely, if not entirely, because of Manning, coming off the greatest offensive season compiled by a quarterback. Manning was the first in history to exceed 5,000 yards passing (5,477) and 50 touchdowns (55).

No team had handled Manning. He threw to eight-to-10 receivers and was difficult to sack—18 times to Wilson's 44—because he got rid of the ball so quickly.

By winning the NFC Championship, Russell Wilson became the sixth quarterback to start a Super Bowl in his first or second season, following Colin Kaepernick (XLVII), Ben Roethlisberger (XL), Tom Brady (XXXVI), Kurt Warner (XXXIV), and Dan Marino (XIX). (Photo by Drew Sellers)

During the regular season, Manning took a league-shortest 2.36 seconds to throw vs. Wilson's league-longest 3.18. More than that, Manning's greatest asset was his ability, manifested best by his gyrating arms and calls of "Omaha," to influence defensive players to move into spots where he wanted them.

"You can't try to be a genie and out-think him," said Seahawks safety Earl Thomas. "So it's best to line up and do what you do."

"We are really up against it," added Pete Carroll.

Manning's Broncos averaged 37.9 points and would face a Seahawks defense that allowed a league-best 14.4. Denver's scoring number was 14.5 higher than the league average. Seattle's scoring defense number was 9.0 better than the league standard. The difference of 23.4 would be the greatest disparity between any two units in Super Bowl history.

In the 10 Super Bowls with the largest statistical disparities between offenses and defenses, the defensive unit won eight times. Further, in the six Super Bowls that matched the No. 1 offense vs. the No. 1 defense, the defense had prevailed five times. But none of those winning defenses had faced a quarterback with Manning's skills. On top of that, the Seahawks would be the second-youngest team to play in a Super Bowl.

And Carroll, at 62 the league's second-oldest coach, had never been to a Super Bowl—as player, coach, fan, guest, or media member.

"Never," Carroll said. "I really had the thought a long time ago that I'm not going until we're playing in it. Fortunately, we're finally going."

Carroll did a remarkable job with the Seahawks, especially in his consistency of word and deed, never letting highs or lows compromise the goal. He managed distractions well and kept his players focused.

None focused quite like Wilson, who spent three hours on the flight to New York studying video of the Broncos defense. Wilson recognized that a key to beating it was to keep it sidelined, meaning that running back Marshawn Lynch and receivers Doug Baldwin, Golden Tate, and Jermaine Kearse would have to be at their best.

"Keeping this game normal is about staying focused on your preparation," Wilson said. "Making sure you're getting sleep. Making sure that you're eating well, making sure you're going through your check list, not being afraid to excel."

During Super Bowl week, one of the 6,329 accredited reporters put a question to Seattle offensive coordinator Darrell Bevell: "Is there a game that's too big for Russell Wilson?" Bevell might have brushed aside the inquiry if not for something he'd noticed in the NFC Championship—a slight case of Wilson nerves. Or was it?

"There was definitely something," Bevell said. "When you look at him or you talk to him, I'm not sure if it was nerves, but we didn't function in some situations. We fumbled on fourth-and-1, and then we fumbled another snap, then we came out the wrong way.

"I'm not putting it all on him because there were other things going on, but we're still talking about a second-year player and that's the first time he had been in that situation.

"I think we need to keep that in mind—we're working with a second-year player. He's fabulous in everything that we've asked him to do. He does a great job of managing situations. He's come up big in just about every one of those for us.

"But we don't want to push the limit and ask him to do too much and have that show up in his play. I don't know if you could do that to him, because he is so well prepared and puts so much pressure on himself to do the right things. But he's showed up big in all of the situations for us."

But even Bevell acknowledged that the Super Bowl was like no other situation Wilson would have experienced. ■

Russell Wilson averaged six yards per carry in 2013 as he led the Seahawks to the playoffs for the third time in four years under head coach Pete Carroll. (Photo by Drew McKenzie)

43–8: SEAHAWKS KNEW IT ALL ALONG

No. 1 Offense Had No Chance Vs. No. 1 Defense

Super Bowl Sunday morning arrived a little cloudy, a little cool, no precipitation, no wind—a benign, Seattle-like start to what would be the longest day in the sports lives of the Seahawks and Broncos. Mike Holmgren, the coach of the only other Seattle team to make a Super Bowl appearance (XL in Detroit), knew all about Super Bowl Sunday. Holmgren had three championship rings—two as offensive coordinator of San Francisco (XXIII and XXIV) and one as a head coach from XXXI when Green Bay defeated New England 35–21.

Holmgren described Super Bowl Sunday as an experience unlike any other: "Coaches like to talk that every game is the same, but the Super Bowl is different. Your emotions are different, your sleep is different, how you pet the dog is different.

"Human beings are in a very stressful situation with a lot at stake. The game starts at 6:30 PM (Eastern). That's one of the bigger challenges. When do we eat? How late do I sleep in? We're all used to games at 1 o'clock. Your clock is important, and it's different."

Although Pete Carroll saw Super Bowls on TV, he was acutely aware of Holmgren's message, making his XLVIII task simple in concept, tough to implement: Keep an abnormal day as normal as possible. That task began as soon as the Seahawks punched their ticket by defeating San Francisco in the NFC Championship. It had two parts.

First, Carroll and his staff had to demystify Peyton Manning and conjure a defensive game plan that took away, or at least dramatically reduced, his unparalleled ability to complete crossing patterns, especially to slot receiver Wes Welker and Demaryius Thomas. Those throws accounted for many of Manning's 5,477 passing yards, ate clock, wore down defenses, and often ended in scores.

Carroll also had to convince 53 players that they not only could—and would—win, but that they would destroy Manning and the Broncos. That became a team-wide expectation regardless of what the media opined or oddsmakers predicted. Carroll was always vigilant in maintaining a constancy in words and deeds and he didn't vary the message for XLVIII.

"Just trying to stay the same," he said in the hours before kickoff. "We've had a strong couple of years here and have played with a really good mindset. I don't want that to change. We're really trying to do the things we always do.…Stay true to ourselves. If we do that, we'll be okay."

Ignoring no detail, Carroll even bothered to choose the same uniform combo—white jerseys, blue pants—that the Seahawks wore December 15 when they defeated the Giants 23–0 at MetLife Stadium.

Carroll plotted everything perfectly. By the end of XLVIII, as a blizzard of blue and green confetti clogged

Russell Wilson hoists the Lombardi Trophy after the Seahawks' dominant 43–8 win over the Denver Broncos in Super Bowl XLVIII. (AP Images)

MetLife Stadium, the Seahawks had crushed Manning and the Broncos so utterly—43–8—that the future Hall of Famer seemed in shock. In fact, Manning appeared bewildered throughout. Nothing he did worked. Manning had never been involved in a big-stage game when so few things went according to plan.

"My hat's off to Peyton Manning and all that he's accomplished," said wide receiver Percy Harvin. "But our defense was looking at that and champing at the bit to get on the field against him."

The Seahawks set a Super Bowl record for fastest score. They set a Super Bowl record with 36 consecutive points to start a game (old mark 24). To put a sly point on it, they scored 12 seconds into the first half and 12 into the second, symbolism for the long-suffering 12s that seemed to go beyond coincidence. And to put an even finer point on that, it was 2–0, 5–0, 8–0, and 15–0 before the Broncos, the most prolific single-season offense in the history of the NFL, finally picked up a first down five minutes into the second quarter.

Undaunted, Seattle linebacker Malcolm Smith picked off Manning at 3:21 of the second quarter, returning the theft 69 yards to make it 22–0. At that point, Manning had a passer rating of 43.6. The 22–0 score at intermission marked the first time a team had pitched a first-half shutout in a Super Bowl since the Baltimore Ravens went up 10–0 on the New York Giants in Super Bowl XXXV.

When Harvin, having had three weeks to clear the cobwebs from a concussion suffered against New Orleans in the divisional round, returned the second-half kickoff 87 yards to make it 29–0, championship fireworks started in Seattle for the first time in 35 years.

Given the respect in which Manning was held, it seemed a little too early to declare victory, but XLVIII was in fact over early. One play in particular—not the safety

12 seconds into the game when Manning and his center, Manuel Ramirez, miscommunicated, giving Seattle its first score—proved decisive. It came on the next Broncos possession, five minutes later.

Manning completed a two-yard pass over the middle to Thomas, who abruptly found himself blasted off his feet by Kam Chancellor, chief boomer in the Legion of Boom. Chancellor's thunderbolt told safety Earl Thomas that the game was over.

"It set the tone," Thomas said. "After that, we knew we would win."

The Seahawks made a mockery of Denver's No. 1 offense by pressuring Manning on the edges and rarely letting him get comfortable. Manning threw for 280 yards, far below his average, and had a passer rating of 73.5, vs. 115.0 in the regular season. The Seahawks also blanketed Manning's receivers downfield and eliminated Denver's running game, holding the Broncos to 27 yards on the ground.

Fans, viewers, and advertisers who settled in for the drama the Super Bowl produced in recent seasons were left instead to ponder the immensity between the Seahawks and the rest of the NFL.

That was a tribute to Carroll, whose vision, enthusiasm, and strategic skill directed a franchise to its first NFL championship—and first in 19 years from a team in the Pacific time zone. He did it in a town where he had been fired 20 years earlier after a single season.

Carroll did it with some players that had pedigree but were mostly mutt, with a few vets but were mostly kids. He did it with the no-respect card that would never be credibly used again with this team, or probably any of his teams. So much for Carroll's rah-rah approach not working in the NFL, whatever rah-rah meant.

As 111.1 million people, the largest audience in American television history, watched the drubbing mount,

Russell Wilson proved to be the perfect fit for Pete Carroll's attack, leading the Seahawks to the Super Bowl XLVIII title in Wilson's second pro season. (AP Images)

as the Seahawks set a Super Bowl record for the variety of their scores—rushing touchdown (Marshawn Lynch), passing touchdown (Wilson 23 yards to Jermaine Kearse, 10 to Doug Baldwin), kickoff return (Harvin), interception return (Smith), field goal (Steven Hauschka), and safety (Cliff Avril)—the question turned to the MVP, often a clear-cut choice.

Not so in XLVIII. It went to Smith, who came to the Seahawks as a seventh-round pick out of USC in 2011, for his 69-yard, first-half interception return, a fumble recovery, and half-dozen tackles.

It could have gone to Harvin for jolting the masses with his kickoff return touchdown and two rushes for 45 yards, the first for 30 that set up the first of Hauschka's two field goals. The MVP could have gone to Kearse, who broke five tackles en route to a 23-yard touchdown catch, or to Baldwin, who had five catches for 66 yards and juked two Broncos' defenders at the goal line on his 10-yard score.

Chancellor would have been a deserving MVP for setting the tone with his hit on Thomas and subsequent interception of Manning. Of course, Russell Wilson easily could have been escorted to Disney World.

Wilson threw a pair of touchdown passes, completed 18-of-25 passes for 206 yards, and finished with a 123.1 rating. He was the third-youngest quarterback (25 years, 65 days) to win a Super Bowl and the fourth second-year quarterback to do so. As Wilson had frequently said, and it was never truer, "Separation is in the preparation."

Earl Thomas agreed.

"Russell Wilson keeps beating all these 'elite' quarterbacks," Thomas said. "Last year he beat Aaron Rodgers and Tom Brady. This year he beat Drew Brees (twice) and Peyton Manning on the biggest stages when it really counted. People need to start putting Russell Wilson in that category because he is an elite NFL quarterback. He's been a pro since day one and he's more than half of why we're winning."

"At the beginning of the season I said to the guys, 'Why not us?'" Wilson remarked in the afterglow. "As the season went on, we continued to grow together and we ended it with a great team win. We had relentless defense, we had Percy Harvin on the kickoff return, our offense was clicking on all cylinders. We got here because we wanted to be champions every day and we brought it every day."

The Seahawks scored 21 points off four takeaways and didn't commit a turnover. But that was the effect, not the cause. For Seahawks players, the drama unfolded exactly as they planned.

"To be honest with you, a lot of the players on this team expected this to be a dominant win," said Baldwin. "I say that with no disrespect to the Broncos. They probably thought that too; that's how you get to a championship game. But the way we prepared, there was no doubt in my mind. You saw us dominate defensively, force the pace on the ground, then make plays in passing game."

Carroll made the Seahawks believe they would shred the Broncos. While the world blinked and stared in amazement at the MetLife Stadium scoreboard that read Seahawks 43, Broncos 8, the Seahawks walked onto the world's biggest stage as if they owned it down to the last bit of confetti.

"It took us four years to get to this point, but we've never taken a step sideways or a step backward," Carroll said. "These guys would not take anything less than winning this ball game. There was not a question in their minds that we wouldn't perform like this." ■

Russell Wilson completed 18 of 25 passes for 226 yards and two touchdowns against the Denver Broncos in Super Bowl XLVIII. (AP Images)

COLD DAY, WARM HEARTS

"Over the Top" Seattle Parade Is Group Hug for 700,000 12s

Every sports market deserves one. But none will ever do a parade quite like Seattle did four days after the Seahawks collected their first Vince Lombardi Trophy.

"I can't imagine one better than that," said head coach Pete Carroll. "That was over the top."

Police estimated 700,000, Seahawks owner Paul Allen countered with a million. But measurement was not about quantity. It was about quality. From babies to oldies, happiness raged as a procession of vehicles transported Seahawks players and coaches from the base of the Space Needle, still topped with a gigantic 12th Man flag, past Westlake Center downtown, along Fourth Avenue into Pioneer Square, and finally to the SoDo stadium district.

At the northern edge, the Mariners opened Safeco Field so that fans could watch free on big screen the culmination of the parade and subsequent welcoming ceremony for players and coaches at the Clink, just to the north. Both facilities were nearly full.

The processional, late getting started, advanced slowly in bitterly cold weather (21 degrees, windchill of 10). Some fans came from Alaska, others from Canada, Montana, Idaho, Oregon. One guy had walked to Seattle from suburban Bellevue over the I-90 bridge.

With every hotel room in Seattle sold out, some people slept in tents on Fourth Avenue concrete as running back Marshawn Lynch stood on a vehicle hood and fired bag after bag of Skittles into the clapping crowd. Russell Wilson, who ignited the team that owner Paul Allen had saved and Carroll remade, happily hoisted the Vince Lombardi Trophy

for much of the 2.5-mile parade route.

"The thing that struck me was the little kids," Carroll said. "Some were screaming and hollering, some were a little intimidated. But they had this moment, and will remember this connection with their parents."

People who witnessed as youngsters a similar Seattle parade in June 1979, a gathering of 300,000 that assembled to fete the NBA champion SuperSonics, could tell you where they stood, which Sonics they saw, how the air smelled, and how they met their spouse that day. For a new generation, the same things happened again.

After the parade turned into the north lot of CenturyLink, players, coaches, executives and staffers clambered down from their vehicles and entered the stadium, where 45,000 season ticket holders hailed their arrival. Introduced by descending numbers, the final player was No. 3, Russell Wilson, who walked onto the field pumping the Lombardi Trophy into the air.

"Our plan is to win another one for you next year," Wilson said.

Although hundreds of thousands gathered, police reported not a single arrest was made. That reminded some of Carroll's comment at MetLife Stadium following XLVIII:

"It was perfect; exactly how it was supposed to go."

How many times in any endeavor can such a thing be said? That is why so many endured such cold to watch a majestic slice of Seattle history parade past: They wanted to celebrate a thing, a thing many had never seen and might never see again, that went exactly as it was supposed to go. A fairy tale came true. ■

Russell Wilson waves beads in the air during the parade in Seattle celebrating the Seahawks' Super Bowl triumph. An estimated 700,000 fans came out for the parade. (AP Images)

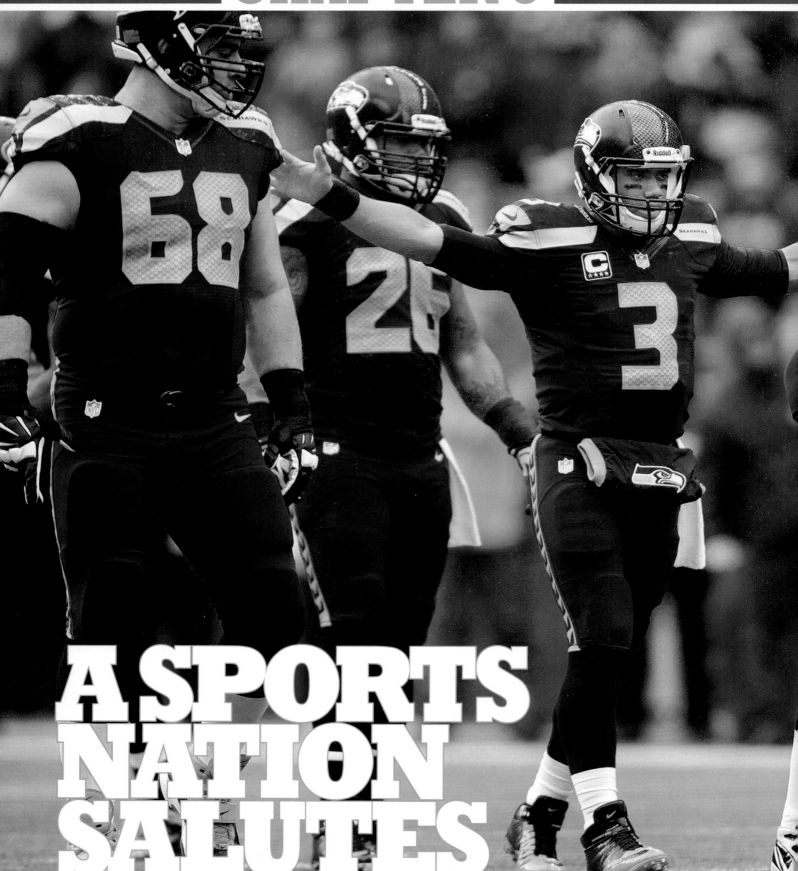

CHAPTER 9

A SPORTS NATION SALUTES

"Every game, I want to improve, to where I have total command of the game and all situations. To be clutch, to be dominant, when I need to be. That's a great way to measure success." – Russell Wilson. (Photo by Drew Sellers)

THE HEIGHT OF SPORTS ACHIEVEMENT

Wilson Enjoys Unprecedented Success in First Two Seasons

After watching his team capture the most prestigious trophy in American sports in the media capital of the world, Seahawks general manager John Schneider ran across the confetti-strewn MetLife Stadium stage in New Jersey and playfully grabbed quarterback Russell Wilson.

"Us short guys," said the 5'7" Schneider to the 5'11" Wilson, "can do it, too!"

Indeed, they could. As can tall cornerbacks. And 330-pound defensive ends. And seventh-round draft choices. And guys whom no teams wanted at all. And twice-fired coaches.

The Seahawks weren't all mutts. But together, they became purebred champions, 43–8 winners over the Denver Broncos in one of the most dominating displays in the XLVIII-year history of the Super Bowl. Central to the first NFL championship in Seattle's history was Wilson, who shattered the Broncos as well as the NFL's bias against short quarterbacks with a masterful performance—his QB rating (123.1) was the ninth-best in Super Bowl annals—in front of the largest audience in U.S. television history.

"I thought it was just an exquisite effort by the quarterback," said coach Pete Carroll, the twice-fired coach. "His play was perfectly fitted to our football team and the plan that we needed to win. It couldn't have been more obvious than it was in the Super Bowl."

Astonished as was the sports world at the breadth and depth of the beatdown, Wilson was not. Throughout his sports career, his deeds defied conventional wisdom and skewered skeptics. Even after his rookie year ended in defeat, he was certain success was near.

"Ever since we lost against Atlanta in the playoffs I remember having that good feeling like, 'Man, we are going to go to the Super Bowl,'" he told the world February 2 on the post-game stage. "It all started with the championship offseason that we had, and just going into training camp and having that mentality of a championship, day after day."

But as often as Wilson cited the word "championship," it is not an end, merely a benchmark.

"As an individual, you want to grow," he said in a quiet conversation after the excitement over the city's first major pro championship in 35 years had turned sublime. "That's my mindset. I want to be consistently progressing, from week one of my rookie year. Every game, I want to improve, to where I have total command of the game and all situations.

"That's a great way to measure success."

Sports championships are always subject to the vagaries of money, health, and luck. Wilson understood that trophies are an emblem of success, not the ultimate validation of a player's worthiness.

Nor does he believe that football success determines the value of the individual.

"A lot of people think football is my life, what defines me," he said. "It's not. For me, faith is No. 1, then football, then helping people where I can. I play better when I can

Only Hall of Famer Dan Marino (six) produced more games with three touchdowns and no interceptions in the first two seasons of a career than Russell Wilson. (Photo by Drew Sellers)

enjoy the people around me, and in the community. It makes a difference when you're helping others."

Not long after Wilson was drafted from the University of Wisconsin, he and his wife, Ashton, moved across the country to the NFL's most remote outpost, where they had no connections. Wilson made one quickly—Seattle Children's Hospital.

A world-renowned pediatric care facility with 250 beds, Wilson began visiting quietly on Tuesdays, typically the off day for players during the season.

For patient and visitor, hospitals are difficult places. They can be particularly so for some professional athletes, usually the perambulating paradigms of good health who can become uncomfortable with scenes of vulnerability. Again, Wilson found a way.

While at North Carolina State, Wilson became used to hospitals because his father, Harrison Wilson, was a diabetic whose complications required increasing hospitalizations.

"I've been in hospitals a lot," he said. "My dad was extremely sick at the time, so (the environment) was comfortable for me. I knew that (in coming to Seattle) I could try to find a way to affect people's lives, but also let them affect my life, and be a positive change."

Harrison Wilson was Russell's idol—a two-sport athlete at Dartmouth College who went on to a get a law degree from the University of Virginia and tried out, at 28, for the San Diego Chargers. He conveyed to his son the importance of "the three Ps"—purpose, perseverance, and perspective—that became Russell's handrails through the intense whirlwind of pro sports.

When the elder Wilson died June 9, 2010, at 55, the day after Wilson was drafted in the fourth round by the Colorado Rockies, the shock was profound. But deploying the three Ps grounded Russell. His experiences at Seattle Children's enlightened him.

"This is my home," he said of Seattle. "I want to feel like I'm part of it, to help in any way possible. If I can communicate with kids at the hospital—spend 15 minutes with one kid, and share my story with them and hear theirs—they don't realize how much that helps me. It gives me a sense of relief, and puts a smile on my face being around them. Week in and week out, they take burdens off my shoulders."

Wilson's uncommon maturity and energy became evident before his ascent in Seattle. He graduated in three years with a degree in communications from North Carolina State, where he wanted to pursue a pro baseball career while maintaining his amateur status for college football. Under NCAA rules, he was allowed to hire an "adviser," not an agent. He received a referral from his college baseball coach for Mark Rodgers, a Florida-based attorney experienced in athlete representation.

"He called me; I didn't call him," Rodgers said. "I thought that was unusual, and refreshing. I'd drive to pick him up at the school's baseball facility to go to lunch. He's in a suit—he looks like the junior senator from the state of North Carolina.

"Then we go to lunch and he asks the waitress, 'May we please have separate checks?' He knows the NCAA rules. That had never happened to me."

After lunch, Wilson and Rodgers reached a deal. Rodgers reached a conclusion.

"This guy was wired differently," he said. "He already had a professional athlete's mentality; he was also a professional human being."

Rodgers also bore witness to a rare Wilson setback. The football coach at N.C. State, Tom O'Brien, wanted Wilson to play spring football in advance of his senior season of 2011. But Wilson, who already had one summer of Class A baseball, wanted a second. If that were the case, O'Brien said, that meant the Wolfpack, despite Wilson's three years of accomplishments, would go in another direction for a starting quarterback—backup Mike Glennon. Each man stood his ground.

"I don't think anyone begrudged the decision, but it was

Russell Wilson threw 52 regular-season touchdown passes in his first two seasons, matching Peyton Manning's NFL record. (Photo by Drew McKenzie)

hurtful," Rodgers said. "There was a sense of rejection. But he's always believed that 10 percent of life is what happens, and 90 percent is how you deal with what happens.

"He's the kind of guy who, when it rains, doesn't get wet."

Because Wilson graduated, NCAA rules allowed him to transfer for his senior year without the mandatory one-year sit-out. After his baseball career continued slowly—a second baseman, he hit .228 in 61 games for the Class A Ashville (N.C.) Tourists—Wilson decided to switch back to college football.

His college transfer choice came down to Wisconsin over Auburn. He left baseball on June 27 and by the end of July had absorbed the Badgers' playbook and was voted team captain. By early December, the Badgers were 10–2, Wilson was the All-Big Ten Conference QB and set the single-season FBS record for passing efficiency (191.8). Wisconsin won the inaugural Big Ten championship game 42–39 over Michigan State, and lost the Rose Bowl 45–38 to the Oregon Ducks.

Wilson's trail of success was followed closely by Schneider, who prior to the April 2012 draft signed the Seahawks' purported quarterback of the future, Matt Flynn, to a veteran free agent contract. But Schneider became enamored of Wilson's leadership and skills despite knowing how few quarterbacks six feet and under succeeded long-term in the NFL, where rules forbid footstools in the pocket.

Wilson's college feats were by no means a secret in the NFL. Every team with needs at quarterback was intrigued. It was a question of which team had the guts to take a chance above a seventh-round pick. Even Carroll was skeptical.

"John convinced me on Russell," Carroll told SI.com. "He was on him early, then he came back from seeing him late in his season at Wisconsin. He was so enthused about him. I watched a lot of tape on him, and John was right on. Then he got here, and he was everything John said he was."

What Wilson was, was more successful in his first two years (24 regular-season wins) than any QB in NFL history. Then the Seahawks in the playoffs beat New Orleans, San Francisco, and Denver, arguably the next three best teams. Such success from nowhere was astounding even to the co-founder of Microsoft, Paul Allen, who knows a little about making something from nothing.

The owner of the Seahawks also had to be persuaded about expending a third-round pick on such an atypical player.

"All the credit goes to John," Allen said after the Super Bowl. "He said there's a quarterback that I really like, and I think he's going to be there. He explained (his height) but said he had everything else you would look for in a quarterback. And now he's a Super Bowl champion.

"I'm just so happy for Russell. To able to do it in his second year is a testament not only to his skill, but all the study of the game's minutiae that he put in to get over the top."

The only two to whom the success was no surprise was Harrison Wilson and his son.

"My dad always told me, 'Russ, why not you?'" he said. "That meant to believe in yourself, believe in the talent God has given you, even though you are 5'11". You can go a long way.

"That's why I decided to play football. I wanted to go against the odds a little bit."

Now the odds grow steeper still—a repeat title. Hasn't been done in a decade. But Seahawks were the youngest team to win a Super Bowl (average age 26.1 years), and know that Wilson is fully capable of getting better.

"We go into this next offseason, and my hopes are that he's really going to take another big step forward and continue to get better," Carroll said. "He doesn't give (opponents) the football. He already understands that.

"His production, his use of the players and the system, will grow. It will allow us to do some really cool things."

As Schneider said, the little guys can do it—again. ∎

This story first appeared in Alaska Airlines Magazine

Russell Wilson won 15 of his first 16 games at CenturyLink Field, the most by a quarterback at home in the first two seasons of a career. (Photo by Drew McKenzie)

TOAST OF MANY TOWNS

Seahawks Leader Becomes Pop-Culture Icon

During a May 21, 2014, White House ceremony saluting the champions of Super Bowl XLVIII, President Obama elicited cheers and chuckles from an East Room throng for his intimate knowledge of the Seahawks. Obama first disclosed the absence of running back Marshawn Lynch, the team's only no-show.

"I wish he was here. I just wanted to say how much I admired his approach to the press," Obama said, referring to Lynch's notorious media shyness. "I wanted to get some tips from him."

The White House show wasn't Lynch's style, even if it marked the final get-together for the 2013 Seahawks. For everyone else, it was a celebration of the pinnacle of American team sports achievement, particularly the Twelves, the Northwest's manic fan base.

For them, the Seahawks offered a nice touch. Rather than give Obama the traditional team jersey with his name on the back, they presented him with a 12th Man flag.

Obama singled out defensive tackle Brandon Mebane's belly roll sack dance ("you can't do that in the White House"), Russell Wilson's newly shaved head ("he looks OK—he doesn't have a peanut head"), Richard Sherman ("We'd give him the mic, but we gotta go in a little bit"), the Seahawks receivers being called pedestrian in a national story ("That made 'Angry Doug Baldwin' even angrier"), and the team swagger ("We don't have to tell you…they do a pretty good job themselves").

On a serious note, Obama mentioned Wilson's becoming the second African-American quarterback to win a Super Bowl, "and the best thing about it was nobody commented on it," as well as the team's relative lack of pedigree: "It excites me when the whole is greater than the sum of its parts."

While that described the 2013 Seahawks, one part still stood out. Russell Wilson had covered the distance from runt underdog to East Room honoree in just two years.

Suddenly a celebrity to go with his status as America's most talked-about quarterback, Wilson became a man in demand following the dismantling of the Broncos, first making two return trips to New York in the days following XLVIII.

He appeared on the *Late Show With David Letterman* on CBS, returned to Seattle, and flew back to New York for an interview on *Late Night With Seth Meyers* on NBC.

After a few preliminaries, Meyers asked Wilson if it was true that he once attended a football camp—the Louisiana-based "Manning Passing Academy"—run by Archie, Cooper, Peyton, and Eli Manning. Wilson smiled, a little sheepishly.

Wilson: "I did."

Meyers: "How old were you when you went to Peyton's camp?"

Wilson: "I was going into the 10th grade, and he actually was my quarterback coach . . . that's kind of eerie."

Meyers: "He was probably on the sidelines (at the Super Bowl) saying, 'Why did I teach him all these things!'"

Wilson: "Going through the draft process, you go to all these different teams and check out different places. The last

Russell Wilson was a guest on the *Late Show* with David Letterman after the Seahawks' Super Bowl win. (Getty Images)

place I went to was the Denver Broncos, and Peyton Manning was there in the locker room going through his notes. I introduced myself.

"Peyton said, 'Don't I know you from somewhere?'

"I was kind of embarrassed. I said, 'To be honest with you, you coached me at your camp,' and he just started dying laughing."

Wilson related his story a week before NFL.com announced that Wilson's No. 3 had become the top-selling jersey in the NFL, eclipsing Manning's No. 18 (one headline stated, "Hotcakes selling like Wilson jerseys"). Wilson nabbed the top spot partly due to his engaging personally, but mostly because of his performance.

- Wilson was the only quarterback in history to post a passer rating of 100.0 or higher in each of first two seasons.

- With 52 touchdown passes, Wilson tied Manning for second-most in the two seasons. The touchdowns came—not the case with Manning, Dan Marino, or many of the rest—with a team oriented to run more than pass.

- Wilson's 24 regular-season victories ranked No. 1 among quarterbacks in the first two seasons (dating to 1970).

- His 15 home victories were most by a player in the first two seasons by a quarterback in the Super Bowl era (since 1966).

- His 10 fourth-quarter comebacks through two seasons were second-most since 1970.

- His 100.6 career rating ranked first in Seahawks history, as did his 63.3 career completion percentage.

All of that and more was why Wilson was suddenly A-List.

He sat courtside at a Brooklyn Nets game, chatting up Jay-Z and Beyonce. He shot a cameo for the *Entourage* movie. He shot a commercial for Microsoft promoting its Surface Pro 2 tablet. He signed an endorsement deal with American Family Insurance, appearing in an ad that encouraged viewers to pursue their dreams.

Wilson made *Access Hollywood* for turning down offers to appear on *Dancing with the Stars*. He spoke to North Carolina State players before their spring football game in Raleigh.

The Texas Rangers, who obtained Wilson's baseball rights in the December 12, 2013 Rule V draft, invited Wilson to throw out the ceremonial first pitch before their April 3 game against the Philadelphia Phillies. Wilson and several teammates also threw out the first pitch when the Mariners opened their home season against the Los Angeles Angels at Safeco Field.

Wilson's relentless belief, backed by historic play, was why he was a leader. The rest of his world followed, happily.

Indefatigable. Resourceful. Visionary. Unflappable. But not even Pete Carroll, the human adjective factory, could finish the description.

"There is no way I can describe the amount of what he does," Carroll said. "He's just an amazing kid. He is just good."

Wilson also made each day, as he liked to say, "a championship opportunity," perhaps the real secret to his success. ■

The Super Bowl champion Seahawks were honored by President Barack Obama during a visit to the White House on May 21, 2014. Obama shakes hands with cornerback Richard Sherman while Wilson, to the right of Sherman, looks on. (AP Images)

Russell Wilson won his first 14 games at CenturyLink Field before the Arizona Cardinals defeated Seattle Dec. 22, 2013. (Photo by Drew McKenzie)